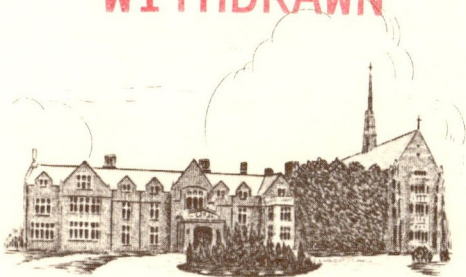

EX LIBRIS

NEWTON COUNTRY DAY SCHOOL OF
THE SACRED HEART

NEWTON   MASS.

Studies in Major Literary Authors

Edited by

William E. Cain
Professor of English
Wellesley College

A Routledge Series

Studies in Major Literary Authors

William E. Cain, General Editor

WILLIAM DEAN HOWELLS
AND THE ENDS OF REALISM

Paul Abeln

Routledge
New York & London

Published in 2005 by
Routledge
270 Madison Avenue
New York, NY 10016
www.routledge-ny.com

Published in Great Britain by
Routledge
2 Park Square
Milton Park, Abingdon
Oxon OX14 4RN
www.routledge.co.uk

10 9 8 7 6 5 4 3 2 1

Abeln, Paul, 1971-
   William Dean Howells and the ends of realism / by Paul Abeln.
      p. cm. -- (Studies in major literary authors ; v. 36)
   Includes bibliographical references.
   ISBN 0-415-97096-2 (alk. paper)
   1. Howells, William Dean, 1837-1920--Criticism and interpretation. 2. Realism in literature. I. Title. II. Series.

PS2037.R37A24 2005
818'.409--dc22

2005018253

Contents

Acknowledgments

This book would not have been possible without the support of my friends, family, and colleagues over the past few years. I want to thank my colleagues and advisors at Washington University, especially Robert Milder, Dan Shea, Steven Zwicker, Robert Weninger and Naomi Lebowitz for their guidance and modeling of good scholarship. So many of the ideas in the book emerged from my many conversations with Matt Devoll, Randy Fuller, and Jen Romney at Dressels. Many thanks to the curators, librarians, and staff at Harvard's Houghton Library for their help and for access to Howells's diaries, journal, and letters. Over the past four years, I have been supported in every way by Barbara Rogers, Kathleen Scully Hodges, and my colleagues at NCDS. I want to express special gratitude to Charles Berman, Erin Royston, Valerie Sullivan, and John Tierney for keeping me sharp and challenging me to grow in all the right ways. Finally, I thank my family for all of their care, interest, and devotion, Clare for her years of love and support, and Lucas for making everything worthwhile.

Introduction

This is always the way . . . that the reformer (perhaps in helpless confession of the weakness he shares with all humankind) champions some error which seems as dear to him as the truth he was born to proclaim . . .
—Howells[1]

In October, 1891, the editors of *The Atlantic Monthly* ran a lengthy review of William Dean Howells's then most recent publication, *Criticism and Fiction*. After the requisite paragraphs paying homage to the journal's former editor and frequent contributor, the review takes a negative turn, indicting Howells for his unconvincing arguments for literary realism and "the incoherence of his protestations" against current literary taste and trend in America.[2] Although this review, among others, faintly echoes the polemics against literary baseness and squalor that had been aimed at Howells in the late 70s and early 80s, by 1891 the shock-value of literary realism had dissipated. Howells was no longer the controversial flag-bearer of an American avant-garde; he had failed to meet the high expectations of a readership seeking more from him and from his fiction than *The Rise of Silas Lapham* and a series of disjointed "Editor's Study" pieces. In short, by the early 1890s Howells had failed to project a stable authorial persona and to offer to his readers a sense of the trajectory of his developing career and intellectual program.

Howells's recent move to New York City in 1888 gave him a degree of what the narrator of *A Hazard of New Fortunes* would describe as the "relief" brought on by "the immunity from acquaintance[. . .]this almost loss of individuality at times, after the intense identification of [his] Boston life."[3] But neither "intense identification" with realism and New England gentility nor "immunity from acquaintance," his feelings of personal and cultural anonymity in New York, produced for Howells the imaginative energies and the confidence he required to reinvent and reassert himself in the 90s. Henry James, ever supportive and competitive, wrote to Howells in 1891: "Your

nomadic ways give me an overwhelming impression of a large free power—
and make me feel like a corpulent fireside cat, tied by a pink ribbon to the
everlastingly same fender." Despite compliment, hyperbole, and mixed in-
tent, James here identifies precisely Howells's crisis in the 1890s: his inability to locate, inhabit, and focus his "large free powers" in a measurable
intellectual space.

Howells's readers, critics, and "fans" articulated the same fond dissatisfaction with him in the 1890s. The *Atlantic* reviewer of *Criticism and Fiction*
closes his essay on a hopeful note: "Far be it from us [the editors of the
Atlantic] to set out on a study of Howells in his first and second periods. How
do we know that there will not be a third which will offer even a better van-
tage-ground for observing the intellectual path made by him?" Hamlin
Garland declared in a New York lecture that "the test of the value of Mr.
Howells's work will come fifty years from now, when his sheaf of novels will
form the most accurate, sympathetic and artistic study of American Society
yet made by an American."[4] This unusual critical posture—the construction
of Howells as a nineteenth-century phenomenon understandable only in an
imagined twentieth-century context—speaks to the utter inability of his
contemporaries to identify the imaginative locus or intellectual direction of
his works.

The term "Realism," seemingly inseparable from Howells's creed and
crusade in the early-to-mid 1880s, had all but disappeared from his texts by
1890. The publication and republication of his partially excerpted 1880s
"Editor's Study" pieces, first in *Criticism and Fiction* (1891), later in *Literature
and Life* (1901), and throughout the twentieth century in anthologies and
schoolbooks, made his comments on literary realism the primary feature of
his legacy. A July 1891 review of *Criticism and Fiction* in *The Nation* cynically
captured the formation and reformation of Howells's legacy: "a few early startling statements attracted great attention, and since then [Howells] has been
the critical sensationalist of the time. His little volume is the record of all this;
but it has no value except as an example of eccentricity."[5]

This study, "William Dean Howells and the Ends of Realism," examines the trajectory of Howells's novelistic career after the transformative success of his most celebrated novel, *The Rise of Silas Lapham*, as a function of his
increasingly perplexed self-identification with and attempts to distance himself from the term "realism." It begins with a single governing idea: Howells
was a writer unsure of his artistic skill, his political stance, the integrity of his
manhood, and the greatness of his America. Only by addressing this fundamental and definitive self-doubt can one begin to understand the unique shape
of his career after 1886, and to pinpoint the moments when his imaginative

locus comes into clearest relief. As Howells began, in the late 1880s and 1890s, to address his own fundamental inability to locate a "common ground" for his emotional, political, imaginative, and professional personas, his fiction became dominated by tropes of miscommunication, misunderstanding, and misperception.

The only recent work to approach Howells's career in a similar fashion is Charles Harmon's "*A Hazard of New Fortunes* and the Reproduction of Liberalism" (*Studies in American Fiction*, Fall 1997). In this article Harmon argues that Howells recognized the force of revolution and revolt at the base of American culture. He claims that the perception of crisis, threat, and fracture is the very motivator and propagator of the American sense of self and national community. For Howells, dramatizing uncertainty, division, diversity, contention, and social fracture created a kind of fuel for ongoing liberal thinking and potential action. Myths or romances of national or dramatic unity, on the other hand, lulled the political and spiritual activist to a dreamy inaction, an intellectual torpor. Just as Howells found his own artistic and political center at moments of personal crisis, so he imagined the country could profit from a literature that enacted fractures of self, family, and class confidence.

It is here that this study breaks from previous readings of Howells. Rather than catalogue crippling psychological events in Howells's career and attribute his unsteady production to them, I read many of his moments of personal crisis as powerful energizers of his fiction. Here I diverge from the works of Cady, Lynn, Bell, Daugherty, Anesko, and others, who often rely on the image of Howells as a victim of historical and biological circumstance. I work rather to describe his professional ambitions, his drive to maintain the integrity of his often unpopular agenda, and his craving for imaginative energies as collectively unsustainable goals.

Even the most rigorous studies of Howells, including Anesko's *Letters, Fictions, Lives* and Bell's *The Problem of American Realism* rely on a set of loosely defined terms to describe the "controlling ideas" of Howells's 1880s and 1890s fiction. Among the most common such terms are "complicity" and "economy," both used extensively by Howells and his critics but neither explained nor illustrated sufficiently in primary or secondary texts. This essential lack of terminological focus must be understood as a legacy of Howells's own disabling uncertainty rather than as a product of poor scholarship. While it may seem as if the immense body of nonfiction that Howells produced in his sixty-year career would provide a lexicon for use alongside his fiction, such works as the "Easy Chair" and the "Editor's Study" often produce the opposite effect: further obscuring our understanding of the novels through layers of social posturing and blurred autobiography.

While "realism," a term easily as perplexing and contested as "complicity" or "economy," stands at the center of our current understanding of Howellsian fiction, it was in fact during Howells's career that the term began to lose its value as a useful signifier for literary *endeavor.* To understand the disenfranchisement of the term, we must historicize it outside of the many theoretical debates that have surrounded it in recent decades: its continuance as a category or rubric for literary study is a secondary concern. Howells's fiction chronicles the rapid transformation of "realism" in America from an emergent signifier of literary modernity in the 1870s and 1880s to a residual, diluted, ineffective, and even disabling aesthetic mode at the turn of the century. Late in his life, Howells would see his legacy linked rhetorically to "realism" and would find himself unable to project a personal or professional image powerful enough to break the connection.[6]

This problematic legacy has remained strongly evident in the most recent scholarship on American literary realism. Donald Pizer, editor of the recently released *Cambridge Companion to American Realism and Naturalism* (1995) and author of *Realism and Naturalism in Nineteenth-Century American Literature* (1966) argues that those writing about "American Literature between the Civil War and World War I" must face three major obstacles: traditional suspicions of literary taxonomy, "the attraction of a deconstructive stance," and New Historicist distrust of historical divisions.[7] Pizer vindicates his and other scholars' attempts to write about realism by claiming to proceed, "despite these difficulties, because of a faith in the value of striving to create threads of shared experience and meaning out of the inchoate mix of life" (1).

It was precisely the "inchoate mix of life" that Howells came to see as the primary driver of the American liberal ideal and his own imaginative production. Especially later in his career, Howells's advocated a poetics of fracture and division—a literature of cultural renewal that sought to expose a moral universe beneath dominant structures of feeling. An extension of his personal quest for an imaginative center and an aesthetic vocabulary accessible to a nation of readers, Howells worked to identify the "common" stuff of American life (material objects, empirical facts) as the only possible conductors of a universal and democratic American discourse. Adopting a Whitmanesque paradigm, he strove to strip away class- or culture-based significations—most specifically those of gilded-age capitalism—by exposing their unreliability.

The clearest examples of such experiments in the location of a democratic language for articulating and defining individual experience appear in Howells's novels of the late 1880s and early 90s. Chapter 1 explores Howells's reevaluation, immediately following the success of *The Rise of Silas Lapham* (1885), of his status as a promoter of literary realism. This chapter, informed by Frederic Jameson's 1982 essay on Balzac, "Realism and Desire," works to address the complex authorial presence (Jameson calls it *fantasm* or *fantasy* element) in the Howellsian novel. Howells's sense of cultural and national duty—"the truth he was born to proclaim"—studied in light of his creative and deeply personal anxieties, suggests a particularly complex authorial dynamic in his texts. Howells's polyvocal 1880s novels enact a narrative of national self-examination on class and an extended fantasy-reconciliation of his confident public persona with his irresolute private fears. Through a careful examination of his 1886 novel, *The Minister's Charge,* and of essays and letters produced concurrently, I hope to demonstrate the ways in which, as early as 1886, Howells's self-identification as a realist becomes increasingly incommensurate with his sense of the role and agency of literary "art."

Chapter 2 examines Howells's fictional treatment of his own reception among the American public. Through his central figure, Basil March, Howells tests the capacity of the middle-class American mind to absorb, assimilate, and resolve the contradictions of social and economic life in the America of the 1890s. March stands as an idealized Howellsian reader: a sensitive critical mind with a generous and liberal social conscience. Confronted with a degree of individual professional success as he witnesses social turmoil, March drifts into and out of his comfortable domestic sphere engaging with the complexities of American life with a mixture of courageous analysis and apathetic withdrawal. The chapter argues that *Hazard* functions simultaneously as a critique of the aesthetic immaturity of the American mind and as an acknowledgement of Howells's own complicity with the social conditions that foster such a state.

The third chapter of this study addresses the conflict between professional advancement and imaginative development that seemingly crippled Howells as a novelist in the 1890s. Drawing on a series of comprehensive studies of the market conditions surrounding him by Daniel Borus, Edwin Cady, Stanley Corkin, Ellen Ballou, and others, I examine the imaginative traffic between Howells's professional and aesthetic personas. It was this very conflict that formed the productive animus at the center of his late career: his craving for success as a literary businessman produced a self-loathing that fueled his desire to attack the trappings of capitalism on the fictional page.

After this pivotal chapter on the marketplace, the project briefly analyzes Howells's retreat in the mid 1890s into psychological, utopian, and eventually autobiographical fiction. Beginning with a discussion of the Altrurian novels, I close the chapter with a reading of Henry James's 1904 lecture "The Lesson of Balzac," a piece which speaks clearly to and about Howells, addressing his conception of and dependency on the limiting concept of "realism," and about the imaginative circumspection that characterized his work throughout the 90s.

The closing chapters of the study address the ways in which Howells gradually moved, between 1890 and 1910, toward a representation of the very incoherence that had characterized his productions during this time. By examining the frontier revivalist rhetoric of the character Dylks in Howells's *The Leatherwood God* (1916), I work to document his surrender of hope for cultural transformation through rational and measured realistic representation of American life. Dylks, a preacher who lays claim to divine rhetoric and authority in a small Ohio town, exercises a power Howells simultaneously admires and decries. The text is an enactment of Bercovitch's *American Jeremiad;* it is an all-but-forgotten Howellsian novel that identifies whim and histrionics—as defined by Emerson on the one hand and Clemens on the other—as the primary drivers of the American intellect. Conceived and produced in the years following the death of Howells's close friend Samuel Clemens, *The Leatherwood God* works to imagine and dissect the ideal of the American author/celebrity. The elegiac tone of the work reinforces the already clear connections between the aging Howells's biographical and fictional efforts. While recasting Howells's critique of the American reader in spiritual terms, *The Leatherwood God* conjures an image of the artist as a charlatan in the tradition of P.T. Barnum whose sense of entitlement frees him of culpability. Here again Howells's looks to the artist with interest and to the crowd with disappointment. His study is made all the more interesting by its proximity—both in time of composition and in mode of expression—to his most celebrated biography, *My Mark Twain.*

In the fifth and final chapter, I read Howells's *The Vacation of the Kelwyns* (1920) and "The Critical Bookstore" as commentaries on the transformations of literary language throughout the later years of his career. Howells spent years writing and revising *Vacation,* first conceived as "The Children of the Summer" in the late 1880s. I analyze the novel as a record of Howells's ebbing confidence in "realism" and as a chronicle of what he perceived to be the collapse of literary discourse as a means of persuasion, mass education, and social reform. It is not only the finished text, published after Howells's death, that I examine, but also the multitude of typescripts, notes, manuscripts, and drafts of the novel now stored at Harvard's Houghton Library. The long period of composition, and Howells's continuing and minute attention to it, allow me to read *The Vacation of the Kelwyns* as a record of his changing confidence in his own ideals and as a measure of his disassociation from (and the implied "vacation" of) "realism."

Prologue
Howells at the Fair

At the peak of his early career, in 1876, Howells turned with much of the nation to focus for a moment on the startling energies of the Philadelphia Centennial Exposition. While the fair stood as a powerful symbol of healing for a nation deeply wounded by war and social unrest, Howells's eye seemed drawn more to its failings than its optimistic and even utopian projections. As he wandered the exposition, recording observations for his July, 1876 *Atlantic Monthly* piece "A Sennight of the Centennial," he looked with some vexation on the composition of the exhibits themselves:

> . . . there are people of culture in this region who would sign a petition asking the government to change the language on the placard on the clothes of the Father of his country, which now reads, 'Coat, Vest, and Pants of George Washington,' whereas it is his honored waistcoat which is meant, and his buckskin breeches: pantaloons were then unknown and 'pants' were undreampt of by a generation which had time to be decent and comely in its speech . . . 1

Though hardly surprising that Howells would notice and criticize the desiccation of American language, his emphasis on the careless disrespect signified by the placard stands as an early example of an anxiety he would revisit throughout his career. The attempt to make Washington accessible to fairgoers strikes Howells as not merely slapdash but dangerous. It is, in fact, the effort to "modernize" Washington, to package him as a late nineteenth-century figure rather than a plain, decent, heroic revolutionary that unnerves Howells and his imagined peers "of culture." Having himself built a career based on the one hand on the veneration and emulation of America's literary establishment and on the other in the myth of the self-made, plain spoken frontiersman,

Howells had little patience for the exhibition's emphasis on mass-production and fad.

In his 1891 essay "On Realism, Criticism, and the Social Effect of Literature," Howells articulates this same response to the caprices of popular taste:

> I understand, that moods and tastes and fashions change; people fancy now this and now that but what is unpretentious and what is true is always beautiful and good and nothing else is so. This is not saying that fantastic and monstrous and artificial things do not please; everybody knows that they do please immensely for a time, and then, after the lapse of a much longer time, they have the charm of the rococo . . . ("On Realism" 69).

The artificiality of the language in the George Washington placard disturbs him because it is inaccurate and "indecent." It is the product of an America that speaks a language of machinery; he laments "the inspired marbles, the breathing canvases, the great literatures; for the present America is voluble in the strong metals. . . ." (96). Howells himself admits to succumbing to "immense, temporary pleasures" and enchantments of the emerging industrial age, most clearly as he gazes at the enormous Corliss Engine, centerpiece of the Centennial displays: "of that first impression the majesty of the great Corliss engine, which drives the infinitely varied machinery, remains most distinct . . . [it] does not lend itself to description . . . In the midst of this ineffably strong mechanism is a chair where the engineer sits reading his newspaper . . . he is like some potent enchanter there, and this prodigious Afreet is his slave who could crush him past all semblance of humanity with his lightest touch" (96). Here to some extent Howells projects an image of himself: the writer/reader helplessly vulnerable in the midst of a thoughtless and monstrous modernity.

Throughout his review of the Exposition, Howells's tone reveals itself to be more sardonic than impressed. "I have just written a mighty long account of the Centennial in the July number," he writes to Mark Twain, "and I shall now hammer away at my comedy."[2] We know from Trachtenberg's report of Howells's elated response to the 1893 Chicago Fair that he had no innate prejudice against such spectacular events: "Howells exempted the Fair from his assaults on selfishness and greed, holding it up as the very model for a better future: 'glorious capitals which will whiten the hills and shores of the east and borderless plains of the west'" (Trachtenberg 218–219). What was it then, about the 1876 Exposition which led him to past celebration to satire?

What Howells found most unnerving about the America of the 1870s—and of the decades following—was what he perceived to be a lack of unity of purpose and ideology. The political, social, and more fundamental ideological fragmentations of the industrial age, while hardly new, presented a powerful and potentially catastrophic challenge to Howells's literary ethos, his hopes for a meaningful "realism," and his sense of himself as a transformative figure in America's literary establishment. The Exposition which he regarded as representing "many ideas besides that of a national festival," defined itself too loosely for his complete approbation. In his review, he eagerly seeks to locate an ideological center:

In this host of heterogeneous humanity, this wilderness of deal boxes of all shapes and sizes, of temples, pavilions, booths, grand pianos, porcelain teacups, flags, chips, shavings, planks, and paint-pots, there were all the elements of an organic chaos, yet an indefinable sense of order predominated, which must have been the mental recognition of a plan as yet invisible in the faintest outline . . . (88).

Howells's enthusiasm rapidly disappears. He, like Whitman, found the anticipation of the Exposition "marvelously curious and attractive" (88). The physical structure of it, and the immense preparation and potential unity it suggested, incited in him a brief and intense hopefulness, which "disappeared in the nature of things as the day of opening approached." (88).

The majority of his "A Sennight at the Centennial" catalogues what Howells considers to be a predominantly hilarious assemblage of national and international bric-a-brac. He describes an Italian sculpture of Washington perched on a soaring eagle: "the eagle life-size and the Washington some six-feet high from the middle up; having no occasion for legs in the attitude chosen, Washington thriftily dispenses of them" (93). Other descriptions of "foreign contributions" to the Exposition are equally biting, particularly that of a mechanized sculpture of Cleopatra "who rolls her head alluringly from side to side . . . for twelve hours every day." The tone of the commentary recalls the tones of Howells's lighter social comedies of the 1870s, which had not yet acquired fully the somber and searching qualities of his later texts.[3]

The Howells at the Centennial was by no means the same man who marveled at the order and ideological power of the Chicago Fair, but as such he is a more reliable reporter. Beneath his high-brow tone, Howells seems open to the possibilities of the Exposition. He does "give it a chance" to show him something new, and he searches for some structural or foundational "plan." Unlike the many literary figures who had distanced themselves from the Fair, Howells does not project or imply a protective nostalgia for antebellum America; he looks, rather, for "a sense of purpose amid what looked like a mere riot of inchoate matter" (88). Despite his best attempts, he finds only large, dangerous abstractions temporarily mollifying a nation in profound ideological and economic flux. He does not deny that the abstractions affect him; Howells admits that "no one can see the fair without a thrill of patriotic pride" (107).

The Exposition's inchoate forms and "immense, temporary pleasures" would remain antithetical to Howells's realism throughout his career. And his own response to it, his desire on the one hand to locate meaning and purpose in its busy, clamorous halls, and on the other to resist its voluble emotional appeals, would help him understand the crisis at the center of his literary enterprise. Howells would demand of his readers the same patient encounter with the real—with the stuff of everyday life—that he demanded of himself at the fairs. In the same way, his evolving images of authorship would move from the minister to the teacher to the proselyte: guides whose voices would intensify in the face of an increasingly voluble incipient modernity.

Chapter One

"The Error He Championed":
The Minister's Charge and Howells after
The Rise of Silas Lapham

> Ever the undiscouraged, resolute,
> struggling soul of man;
> (Have former armies fail'd?
> then we send fresh armies—and fresh
> again;)
> Ever the grappled mystery
> if all earth's ages old or new;
> Ever the eager eyes, hurrahs, the welcome clapping-hands, the loud
> applause;
> Ever the soul dissatisfied, curious,
> unconvinced at last;
> Struggling to-day the same—battling the same.
>   — Walt Whitman, "Life," from "Sands at Seventy", 1888

While the Howells of the early twentieth century "Easy Chair" could look back on his younger self with fond dissatisfaction, he was unable or unwilling to recognize the deep structures of dissatisfaction that had seeded themselves in the professional anxieties of the 1880s and found increasingly diverse aesthetic expression over thirty years. Although his more self-conscious devices, particularly images of place or location (homes, towns, resorts), continued to appear with regularity throughout his career, Howells was a writer committed to remodulating his style from project to project. Such reinvention or redirection would, ideally, breathe new life into his theories of realism and prevent the ossification of his ideals which he knew would leave them vulnerable to critical assault and popular withdrawal.

This desire for freshness of style and device also motivated Howells' resistance to the materialism, what he would call "clutter," of the European realistic novel exemplified by Balzac and Zola. Howells, interested far more in the effects of discourse and rhetoric on the middle- class mind than the critique of bourgeois materialism, worked to build into his novels studies of modes of expression determined by class, ethnicity, and geography. Perhaps of greatest interest to him, especially after the reasonable success of *The Rise of Silas Lapham* in 1885, was the potential transformative power of literary language on individual American lives. He would struggle, especially in the late 1880s, with an aesthetic crisis: could literature serve a didactic function while striving to represent the inchoate "mix" of American life—external and internal?

Until 1885, his novels were criticized for their lack of depth and scope. His characters, while drawn with rich detail, lacked the internal life of the most minor Jamesian figure or even Clemens's Huck. Faced with the daunting task of reflecting what Gosse would call "the vast arch of life" with a narrow mirror, Howells struggled to allow his characters even a hint of internal depth.[1] When a morally overwrought and apparently undecided Silas receives the letter from the Great Lacustrine and Polar Railroad near the end of *The Rise of Silas Lapham,* he reads it "mechanically . . . looking blankly at it" (357). Attentive to the rich history of the climactic letter in epistolary, dramatic, and novelistic traditions, Howells uses this scene to reassert and reevaluate a worn-out convention. Here in Lapham the letter carries tremendous force and represents a moment of decision and revelation, but it operates with an agency independent of the web of relationships in the novel. It is mechanical, the product of an industrial growth and expansion unconcerned with the domestic crises of the Laphams and the minor devastations of minor lives.

The potential act of selling the mills, an act that involved "baffling and perplexing" moral consequences, left Lapham feeling that he was involved in "a deeper game than [he] was used to" (349). By deferring his decision until the arrival of the letter, Lapham admits his intellectual and moral inability to participate in the game at all. Rather than act and produce immeasurable consequences, Lapham withdraws into a personal failure that is perfectly measurable, taking with him only his family and the desperately ambitious Rogers. Even his withdrawal is largely an accident, the product of the serendipitous arrival of the GL&P letter, "the verification of his prophetic fear, which was also his sole hope" (357).

That the arrival of the letter represents a *felix culpa* for Lapham—or more precisely an expensive liberation from morally dubious consequences—seems more understandable as a function of Howells' own uncertainty about the consequences of his art. As Lapham helplessly and mechanically reads his own fate, so Howells begins to realize the "deeper game" within his own increasingly ambitious literary projects during the 1880s.[2] Pressured on one side by his lifelong effort to produce culturally relevant and socially productive texts in the tradition of Emerson and Whitman and on the other by the Jamesian impulse to "move in a diviner air," Howells formulates his realism with a troubled faith in a novel's capacity to engage with cultural forces well beyond the scope and understanding of any one author, politician, or social philosopher. [3]

Howells' "prophetic fear" involved the impossibility of meaningful individual thought and action in a republic that had outgrown—through population growth, immigration, industrialization, and incorporation—an idealized liberal democracy. To address a cultural aristocracy as Emerson had in his "American Scholar"; to imagine a great national self in which "every atom belonging to me as good belongs to you" as Whitman had in *Song of Myself;* both seemed disingenuous in the America of the 1880s. Could one of Howells' middle-class readers imagine him—or, more likely, her—self engaged in culturally transformative action or even in the kind of heroic self-culture enacted by Thoreau?

These doubts extended for Howells from his own fear that his developing self-identification with both the terms "realist" and "reformer," and his attempts to broaden these private tendencies to public literary trends, were products of what he considered his psychological flaws and inadequacies. At the end of the decade, in an 1889 review of Walt Whitman's *November Boughs,* he would express this worry in a fairly typical moment of self-reflection:

> [Whitman] made it possible for poetry hereafter to be more direct and natural than hitherto; the hearing which he has braved nearly half a century of contumely and mockery to win would now be granted on very different terms to a man of his greatness. *This is always the way; and it is always the way that the reformer (perhaps in helpless confession of the weakness he shares with all humankind) champions some error which seems as dear to him as the truth he was born to proclaim . . .* (emphasis mine)[4]

This somewhat ambivalent explanation of Whitman's erotic excesses speaks to Howells's sense of the force of his own "weaknesses" in the development of his signature mode of representation: the realistic novel.

The 1880s may have been Howells most remarkable period of creative production, but it was also—not surprisingly—his most personally trying. He suffered a nervous breakdown in 1881 following his resignation of the

Atlantic editorship; his daughter Winifred began a tragic descent into what a number of contemporary biographers, including Michael Anesko, have diagnosed in hindsight as a severe case of *anorexia nervosa.* In 1886 and 1887, following the initial successes of *A Modern Instance* and *The Rise of Silas Lapham*, he felt his social and personal values and his faith in American democracy threatened by the jailing of the Haymarket "anarchists." His move to New York in 1888 has often been identified as a pivotal moment of transformation in his life and career, but its significance dims in comparison to the impact of Winifred's death on March 3, 1889.

Read alongside this line of personal and domestic upheavals, the trajectory of Howells's prose—from the personal degradation of Bartley Hubbard in *A Modern Instance* (1881) to the almost lyrical lightness of *April Hopes* (1889)—surprisingly suggests an increasingly defiant optimism. The brightening light of Howells's realism—so divergent from the broader American and Continental trends toward a grittier positivism—becomes clearer still when he defines it in *Criticism and Fiction* against the shadowy morality of Dostoevsky, and has the chronically miserable reformer Lindau translating that same author in *A Hazard of New Fortunes* (1890).

It was "democracy"—a term with instant American market appeal then and now—that allowed Howells, in his early attempts to formulate a realist poetic, to make logical leaps that concealed and effectively effaced the deeply personal psychological vectors of his creative growth. Michael Bell argues convincingly in *The Problem of American Realism* (1993) that Howells knew his use of popular political rationale—the very word "democracy"—to legitimize realism "was built on sand." "Howells's assertion," Bell argues, "that realism was 'democracy in literature' makes perfect sense as a kind of public relations gesture,

> in the manner of Whitman's assertion at the end of *Leaves of Grass* that the 'proof of a poet is that the country absorbs him as affectionately as he has absorbed it . . . ' Even more important for both Howells and Whitman, clearly, were the psychological benefits of the pose of 'democratic' writer: as against the conventional notion of the irrelevance of literary activity, this pose gave the writer a sense of 'real' social significance . . . and most important, to associate the writer with what was most normal or ordinary in his audience was to dissociate him from the socially marginal and sexually ambiguous implications of the 'literary' and 'artistic.'[5]

For Howells, though, the value of the "democratic" pose was significantly broader than its popular appeal: it was also a function of his own rise to prominence. In the very years that Howells was writing his most celebrated works and drafting the "Editor's Study" pieces that would later become *Criticism and Fiction* he was already abandoning himself to the paradox of his own position. Although he had built himself a relatively secure station in New England through years of hard work, strategic flattery, and productive friendships, Howells would never forget his status as an outsider. He was, without his editorial rank and his circle of influential friends, a mid-western self-starter with no college degree.

His novels of the 1880s, especially *Lapham, The Minister's Charge,* and *April Hopes,* would largely deal with the drama of the outsider in New England high society. Figures like Lemuel Barker, Dan Mavering, and Silas Lapham were not marginalized, disdained, or rejected by the societies they endeavored to enter; instead they were observed as subjects of curiosity, unknown quantities, given every chance (as Howells was) to earn a position in circles of power, a status that Bromfield Corey would label "ancestor" in *The Minister's Charge.*

Although obviously a subject of some anxiety and personal importance to Howells, his status as an outsider in New England and more acutely (after 1888) in New York City, did not shape his realist poetics so much as it shaped his characterizations of primary male figures in his texts. Perhaps his most sensitive reader and certainly most observant friend, Henry James wrote to Grace Norton years later that he'd "always known that [Howells had] a strange, sad kind of subterraneous crepuscular *alter ego,* a sort of 'down cellar' (where they keep the apples of discord) of gloom and apprehension . . . real as this condition in him is, it is a thing disconnected, in a manner, from his *operative* self." Howells was not only a stranger in New England and New York; he was in fact an outsider to himself, a hyper-productive individual existing in professional worlds that he would endeavor to separate from his personal discord. Steady creative work would always bring him treacherously close to explorations of this detached self; he would therefore avoid it, dizzying himself with an editorial career that would permit precious little time for more risky fiction. Howells sacrifice of art to business was his "prophetic fear and his sole hope."

Insofar as "The Man of Letters as a Man of Business," composed in the first years of the 1890s, can be read as a self-reflective piece and not solely as an invective against journalists, it stands as a record of Howells's growing sense of his own splintered artistic persona. [6] In a passage often overlooked, he slips out of the largely professional tone of the piece into a more wistful voice:

> . . . in the field of realistic fiction, or in what we used to call the novel of manners, a writer can only produce an inferior book at the outset. For

this work he needs experience and observation, not so much of others as of himself, and he will need to know motive and character with such thoroughness and accuracy as he can acquire only through his own heart. A man remains in a measure strange to himself as long as he lives, and the very sources of novelty in his work will be within himself; he can continue to give freshness in no other way than by knowing himself better and better . . .

Here, in a key passage to any understanding of Howellsian realism, he speaks again with the help of Emerson and Whitman, echoing *Song of Myself,* "You shall not look through my eyes either, nor take/ things from me, /You shall listen to all sides and filter them through yourself . . ." (26–29). The very idea that the most powerful observer is the most self-reliant observer, he or she who follows the Emersonian edict "know thyself," drove Howells's creative impulse while at the same time producing a disabling fracture in his developing realistic program. Could the novel perform a moral, didactic function while heroicizing the liberated observer/subject? Was the "novel of manners"—a term Howells equivocates with "realistic fiction" in the passage above—a representational mode that could convey the transformative force of Whitman's verse or Emerson's heavily ministerial rhetoric? These questions would constitute for Howells the "deeper game" that prompted his withdrawal in the 90s and the first decades of the twentieth century into a perplexed autobiography and a series of creatively disabling (if lucrative) journalistic contracts.

1886, the year that labor historians remember as the "Great Upheaval," was remarkably calm for Howells. This is obviously a controversial suggestion: given the hardship of much of the 1880s for him and his family, it would seem unlikely that he could find any respite. Although the Chicago Haymarket riot, arguably the event that had the largest imaginative impact on him, would take place in May, it would leave little trace in his work of that year. In fact, it was in 1886 that Howells wrote his most celebrated and berated "Editor's Study" piece, later to be published in *Criticism and Fiction,* in which he declared that what is "peculiarly" American is "the large, cheerful average of health and success and happy life." Such was Howells's own condition for a brief window during the successful serialization of *Lapham* (1885) and the composition of *The Ministers Charge* (1885–86). His daughter Winifred, so ill for so long, was enjoying a brief window of gradual recovery.[1] Despite some exposure to negative reviews of his fiction—especially among the Boston elite—Howells could be confident in his intellectual and social station; he had the luxury of refusing the Smith professorship at

Harvard in 1886.[2] His son John was preparing to graduate triumphantly from that same school and planning a year of architectural study at the École des Beaux Arts in Paris.

While his biographers have used limited and fragmentary biographical evidence to extrapolate a downward spiral in Howells's psychological state during 1886, this conclusion seems unconvincing when one considers the pattern of self-reinvention that he followed in that year. Even Lynn acknowledges a "new assertiveness" and "determination" in his personal exchanges and a "new boldness of purpose" and "imaginative freedom."[3] It had been only the Spring and Summer of the previous year that Howells had experienced a severe (if vaguely documented) nervous breakdown during which, he would claim to a *Harper's* interviewer in 1895, "the bottom dropped out." Despite this and ensuing self-annihilating moments, Howells would rebound spectacularly, "abruptly deviating from accustomed patterns of behavior," effectively domesticating his literary and philosophical programs. He separated himself and his family from the Boston bramhins and pollution by letting his Beacon Street home and moving to Auburndale, MA. From here he would begin his work on new "Editor's Study" columns and write, revise, and serialize the majority of *The Minister's Charge.*

The year could also be described as one of intense imaginative independence for Howells, a self-reliance he had never experienced before and would never enjoy again. His growing respectability in Boston (belied by harsh reviews but verified by contracts and professional opportunities) liberated him in a sense from the venerable Cambridge and Concord genealogy to which he had paid homage for decades. The recent deaths of Emerson and Longfellow gave Howells the opportunity to engage in some fresh canon-building. Energized by his alliance with Samuel Clemens, Howells would work to usher in his self-declared "communistic era in taste" and endeavor to bridge what Sarah Daugherty has identified as the gap between two American tendencies: the elegant and the histrionic. [4]

Clemens represented freedom to Howells, freedom from the tyranny of taste, from canon, and most interestingly from the psychological and verbal instability that so threatened his "hope for a moral order based on shared values." Despite their friendship, Clemens's *literary* means were ultimately useless to Howells. The tools of the humorist seemed to threaten the very moral seriousness that he worked so consistently to embed in his fiction, and he was careful to maintain a strong divide between optimism and cynical histrionics. If Howells wanted to declare independence from his literary progenitors, he wished very much to sustain and promote the cultivated intelligence that they represented to a nation threatened by widespread cynicism and unrest. For this reason, he would sustain a meaningful ongoing correspondence and friendship with Clemens but allow only tenuous professional connections. "Humorist" was one of the many labels Howells resisted: lacking Clemens's famous and respected wit, Howells knew he had to maintain a veneer of high seriousness in his criticism and fiction. He therefore sought his models and mentors among the less accessible and even anonymous literary pantheons of Europe and czarist Russia.

It would be only one year later (1887) that he would declare in an in-troduction to *Sevastopol* that "[Tolstoy is] precisely the human being with whom at this moment I find myself in the greatest intimacy; not because I know him, but because I know myself through him."[5] *A Hazard of New Fortunes* (1890) and *Annie Kilburn* (1889) would represent the beginning of Tolstoy's heaviest impact on Howells's fiction, an impact that grew to a kind of hero worship.[6] Of the many Russians Howells popularized in American markets (including Turgenev and Dostoevsky), he devoted the most attention to Tolstoy, both privately and publicly. He wrote six pieces on Tolstoy in 1887, prompting Charles Eliot Norton to say that Howells had "a bad case of the Russian measles."[7] But interestingly, Howells's passion for Tolstoy did not base itself in any "new" idea or burst of inspiration. On the contrary, it seems that Tolstoy affected Howells in much the same way that Howells hoped the Russians would affect all American readers: he reinforced, redirected, and re-vitalized beliefs and ideas that Howells already held.

This intellectual infatuation had its roots in Howells's youth. His father, William Cooper, had been an intense and somewhat eccentric Swedenbor-gian. In his journals, Howells remembers having heard, as a child, nightly readings from the bible and from Swedenborg's *Heavenly Arcana*. These texts, along with William Cooper Howells's devotion and intensity, left the young Howells with a practical sense of Christian ethics, religious tolerance, and a drive to peaceful social activism. Tolstoy's repudiation of industrial society, based on Christian tenets, held real meaning for Howells, and the doubts about American capitalism that had surfaced in Howells's early writings sud-denly crystallized after his reading of a number of the Russian's stories and novels.[8] He later wrote of Tolstoy:

> His writings have meant more to me than any other man's . . . It has been his mission to give men a bad conscience, to alarm them in the opinions and conventions in which they rested so comfortably . . . he gave me new criterions, new principles, which, after all, were those that are taught us in our earliest childhood, before we can come to the evil wis-dom of the world. . . . [9]

As the moment just preceding his immersion into Tolstoy and the resultant transformation of his fiction, 1886 stands as a year in which Howells evaluated his own "criteria" and "principles" and found them wanting, or at best hopelessly tangled. Written under the profound glare and high expectations produced by the success of *The Rise of Silas Lapham* and serialized at the height of the Haymarket riot controversy, *The Minister's Charge* represents a pivotal and highly experimental stage in Howells's novelistic development. The book represents the author's increasingly inchoate sense of the direction of his aesthetic program stemming from his struggle to resolve the conflict between his desire for fame and his belief in writing as a vocation.

It is important to note here the complicated publication history of *The Minister's Charge*. Howells began the text in the early 80s, finishing only the frames of partial early chapters. Negotiations among Osgood (Howells's publisher and *de facto* literary agent), Alden (editor of *Harper's Monthly*), and Howells spanned three years, 1883–1886; *The Minister's Charge,* in some form, would have been published before *The Rise of Silas Lapham* and *Indian Summer* had Alden not found it wanting. Wrangling continued over the concept and early manuscripts, at one point involving Clemens's publishing company C.L. Webster and people from *The Century*. In the intervening two years, *Lapham* appeared and *Harper's* decided to take their chances on the already complete manuscript of *Indian Summer* rather than the unknown quantity entitled—at different stages—"my pathetic country boy," "The Country Boy in Boston," "Lemuel Barker," and ultimately, *The Minister's Charge*.[10]

Howells would later claim that neither *Lapham* nor *Charge* but rather *April Hopes* (1888) was the first novel he completed "with the distinct consciousness that he was writing as a realist."[11] It is this moment of transition from editorial polemicist to self-conscious realist that is enacted in *The Minister's Charge;* its narrative voices are not yet saturated with the rhetoric of Tolstoy's Christian Socialism, not yet enraged to despair by grief, not yet shaken by the Haymarket executions. Its authorial presence is uncertain, splintered, grasping for a new vocabulary. The text lacks the narrative confidence of *Lapham* but does not permit itself the same moral loopholes; Silas's closing words to Sewell from the earlier novel resonate throughout *The Minister's Charge:* "Seems sometime as if it was a hole opened for me and I crept out of it" (394).

As the novel slowly unfolded in monthly installments, James would praise it for "imparting a palpitating interest to common things and unheroic lives . . . to an even higher point [than *Lapham*]."[12] Although James bases his observation on an incomplete reading, he is eager to detect in Howells a more probing imagination; on the very same page as the above comment he subtly criticizes Howells's novels for exhibiting "so constant a study of the actual and so small a perception of evil." In fact, until the publication of *A Hazard of New Fortunes* (1890), James would express only passing interest in Howells's novels.[13] The moment of Conrad's murder in that book, with its ambiguous effects on the sympathies of Dryfoos, suggested to James that Howells had factored "evil" into his study of the "actual" and had reached the moral crises that realistic fiction must explore. Howells disintegrating hopes in his own brand of defiantly optimistic realism earned him the highest praise that James would ever proffer: "The life, the truth, the light, the heat, the breadth & depth & thickness of the *Hazard* are altogether admirable. It seems to me altogether, in abundance, ease & variety, a fresh start for you. . . ."[14]

Reading *The Minister's Charge*, therefore, is comparable to observing a planet positioned between the stronger light of two massive stars. Much of our understanding of Howellsian fiction comes from a century of critical readings of *Lapham* and *Hazard*, but his coming-into-consciousness as a fiction writer was a gradual, experimental process, a slow effort to incorporate his own editorial fiats into a resistant representational mode: the novel of manners. In the 80s he worked—against the powerful opinion of Henry James and his own troubled psyche—to "champion the error" of the culturally transformative realistic novel.

The Minister's Charge is a text obsessed with the repercussions of errors. The narrative opens with the Reverend Sewell's anxious regret about some insincere but well-intended flattery he had offered to Barker, a country boy and aspiring poet from Willoughby Pastures, MA. Sewell's fear that he has committed a serious injustice seems verified when Barker sends him a letter announcing his plan to come to Boston and seek publishers for his work. Fervently composing a sermon to manage his anxiety, Sewell reflects on

> the text, "The tender mercies of the wicked are cruel," in which he taught how great harm could be done by the habit of saying what are called kind things. He showed that this habit arose not from goodness of heart, or from the desire to make others happy, but from the wish to spare one's self the troublesome duty of formulating the truth so that it would perform its heavenly office without wounding those whom it was intended to heal . . . (8)

Like so many of Howells characters, Sewell develops in no single novel but rather through a number of appearances.[15] While *The Minister's Charge* center-stages him, his role in *Lapham* would be fresh in the mind of readers. His word to the Laphams, who had come to Sewell for advice on their daughters' romantic conflict, was to spurn the false ideals that come "from the novels that befool and debauch almost every intelligence" (258). In other words, rather than allow a novelistic moment of tragic heroism—one sister's abandonment of a lover for the sake of the other's happiness—Sewell insists that the *truth* (as unkind as it may be) would minimize suffering for all involved in the end. This is Sewell's insistent belief in *Lapham* and in *Charge,* and obviously it is also an expression of Howells's own hope for realism. *The Minister's Charge* becomes all the more interesting because this postulate fails utterly; what in *Lapham* did seem to bring about a fortunate fall for the figures involved seems less effective for Lemuel Barker. Sewell's flattery of his insufficient literature—a monumental sin in the minister's mind—opens for Barker a world that would have been absolutely inaccessible to him otherwise. He is saved, altogether unexpectedly, by a bit of idealism.

It is easy to argue that Sewell and Barker represent a splintering of the author's own self-image and voice in the text. On the one hand, the aging minister meditates on his imperiled ethics and on the country boy saunters into Boston society, driven at first only by the flattery of an insider and a belief that he could be a writer.[16] In one of the text's richest passages, young Barker's impressions of Boston are filtered through the point of view of the magazine editor Evans:

> Certainly he formed no adequate idea of the avidity and thoroughness with which Lemuel was learning his Boston. It was wholly a public Boston which unfolded itself during the winter to his eager curiosity, and he knew nothing of the social intricacies of which it seems solely to consist for so many of us. To him Boston society was represented by the coteries of homeless sojourners in the St. Albans; Boston life was transacted by the ministers, the lecturers, the public meetings, the concerts, the horse-cars, the policemen, the shop-windows, the newspapers, the theaters, the ships and the docks, the historical landmarks, the charity apparatus.
>
> The effect was a ferment in his mind in which there was nothing clear. It seemed to him that he had to change his opinions every day. He was whirled round and round; he never saw the same object twice the same. He did not know whether he learned or unlearned most. With the pride that comes to youth from the mere novelty of its experiences was mixed a shame for his former ignorance, an exasperation at his inability to grasp their whole meaning . . . (170)

Here Barker predicts the words Howells would write only a few years later in "The Man of Letters as a Man of Business:" "A man remains in a measure strange to himself as long as he lives, and the very sources of novelty in his work will be within himself; he can continue to give freshness in no other way than by knowing himself better and better. . . ." As Barker grows culturally and intellectually he reinvents himself and simultaneously reinvents the Boston around him. His "inability to grasp" the whole meaning of his experiences recalls Lapham's anxious response to the "deeper game." In Howells, a figure without a cultural circle, a scriptural program, or a strong class-based identity is lost in a whirl of uncertain and unreadable significations. Social structures create meaning and lend vocabulary to experiences in Howells; without such structure one is left with a troubled self-reliance, at once the source of "novelty" and the source of "the apples of discord."

Barker is a linguistic and experiential free agent who succeeds rather well, stumbling through Boston with only blind chance and ambition to guide him. While this would seem to represent a fine example of a self-reliant life, Barker's ceaseless confusion and inability to manage intellectually his complicated experiences in Boston suggest that the text is a record of serendipity and not a heroicization of the democratic self. Howellsian realism, as optimistically projected early in the 80s, provided a vocabulary for articulating experience based on democracy, self-confident individualism, and fidelity to common experience. Lemuel Barker, an outsider with only a fragmentary and almost primal sense of the sights and sounds surrounding him in Boston Common, hardly qualifies as self-reliant; his sloppy process of self-discovery leaves little room for meditation on participatory democracy or "common experience." Barker is an embodiment of the irony of Howellsian realism: the perfect package of social hopes and aspirations hopelessly bound by his own long-term personal development, unable to grasp cognitively any connection with the thousands of equally solipsistic Bostonians around him. This and other obstacles to Howells's ideals would emerge first in *Lapham* and would overwhelm *The Minister's Charge*.

Two sermons provide the scaffolding for the novel, and each takes Barker as its unnamed subject. He becomes, quite accidentally, the model for Sewell's and Evans's published sermon on "complicity" at the text's midpoint, a text that both hope will "stand a chance of sticking, like Emerson's 'Compensation'" (161). Evans attributes the inspiration for the sermon to an experience he had with Barker:

> . . . 'The real reason why I wish you to preach this sermon is because I have just been offering a fee to the head waiter at our hotel.'
>
> 'And you feel degraded with him by his acceptance? For it *is* a degradation.'

'No, that's the strangest thing about it. I have a monopoly of the degradation, for he didn't take my dollar.'

'Ah, then a sermon won't help *you!* Why wouldn't he take it?'

'He said he didn't know as he wanted any money he hadn't earned,' said Evans with a touch of mimickry.

The minister started up from his lounging attitude. 'Is his name— Barker?' he asked with unerring prescience.

'Yes,' said Evans . . . (163).

The scene is deceptively simple. Although Evans acknowledges his own wretched complicity with such "shameful transactions," only sentences later suggests to Sewell that the subject of "[complicity] would give the series a tremendous send-off . . . There would be money in it. The thing would make a success in the paper, and you could get somebody to reprint it in pamphlet form" (163). Sewell sees the moral fissures in Evan's proposition: "People don't have these tremendous moral awakenings for nothing" (163), but he ultimately agrees to the project.

At such moments, Howells's hopes in the eighties for American literature's pedagogical agency seem crippled; this is a crisis illustrated as clearly by Barker's prosperous confusion as it is by Sewell's myopic observations on Barker within and outside of his sermons. If Barker is Sewell's "charge"—a moral and personal responsibility—he is also and more crucially an emblem of a broader social crisis of a type with which Sewell is unfamiliar. He has a "habit of seeking to produce a personal rather than a general effect," (a habit that Howells would admit to sharing) and a serious reluctance to expanding the breadth of his messages and his audiences. In fact, among the most difficult decisions for Sewell in the book is the result of Evan's offer to publish his sermon on "complicity." The narrative voice takes on an ironic tone when Sewell meditates on the effects of the publication:

> It not only strengthened Sewell's hold upon the affections of his own congregation, but carried his name beyond Boston, and made him the topic of editorials in the Sunday editions of leading newspapers as far off as Chicago. It struck one of those popular moods of intelligent sympathy when the failure of a large class of underpaid and worthy workers to assert their right to a living wage against a powerful monopoly had sent a thrill of respectful pity through every generous heart in the country . . . (308).

This "thrill of respectful pity," just like the "traces of tears" on the faces of women in his congregation, suggest the ephemeral effects of emotional appeals.

These are not moments of cultural transformation, and these are not words that create, in the minds of readers and listeners, paradigmatic shifts in world-view. They are, rather, the very same emotions that Howells would constantly indict as vestiges of popular and novelistic romanticism.[17]

Crucially, the novel does not assign these emotional effects only to the readers of the published sermons but also to those in close contact with Sewell. Barker's "case," and everything it represents for this Boston coterie, swirls around its subject with virtually no meaningful impact. Significantly, it is while Barker recovers from a carriage accident in the hospital that Sewell, Corey, and Bellingham contemplate his future: "'He must go back to Willoughby Pastures,' Sewell concluded . . . 'If that sort of thing is to go on,' said Corey, 'what is to become of the ancestry of the future *elite* of Boston?'"(301). Barker's own desire to return to his town and to 'live' after "the pattern of Boston" (303) is tolerated by Sewell as a forgivable "lofty ideal," a bit of naïve youthful optimism.

Sewell responds nervously to the publication of his sermon and reacts dubiously to the suggestion that Barker could have been transformed in any meaningful way by his exposure to the swirl of city life. Interaction with public sentiment is as dangerous to the private intellect as any idealistic novel in Sewell's view. This mistrust is the source of his great theological and personal crisis in *The Minister's Charge*. If, as he declares in his final sermon, "only those who had the care of others laid upon them, lived usefully, fruitfully," (309), then he suggests the somewhat paradoxical need to maintain an intellectual self-reliance and a moral self-abandonment to the needs of a larger community.

The achievement of *The Minister's Charge*, however, is not Sewell's rather uneventful intellectual meandering. It is, rather, the stunning resistance of Barker to the will and theory of the Boston coterie that the novel treats with such deference. At the moment of Barker's physical departure from the world of the novel, Sewell bids farewell to him and to his mother:

> Lemuel promised to write as soon as he should be settled, and tell Sewell about his life and work; and Sewell, beyond earshot of his wife, told him he might certainly count upon seeing them at Willoughby in the course of the next summer. They all shook hands many times. Lemuel's mother gave her hand from under the fringe of her shawl, standing bolt upright at arm's length off, and Sewell said it felt like a collection of corn-cobs. (306)

The striking closing image of a woman utterly alien to Sewell, defined completely by his association of her with the land and her rural poverty, suggests to some degree the emptiness of his intellectual musings. He touches her only because of an exceptionally unlikely chain of events, and the experience is remarkably strange to him. The appearance of such people and their children in Sewell's and Corey's Boston is an inevitable as it is theoretically unmanageable. *The Minister's Charge* explores the impossibility of class insularity and laments the loss of such easily readable and definable worlds.

What would seem to be a rather unspectacular sub-narrative—the relationship, engagement, and presumably the failure of Barker and Statira to marry—represents a commentary on the cross-class interaction that lies at the center of the novel and in fact of Howells's intellectual projects in the 80s. In the world of the novel, the institution of marriage stands as the single greatest threat to and the single greatest protection for the reified Boston social structure. The relationship between Barker and Statira—a sick "working girl," given to paroxysms, whose very name is a play on "status" and "satire"—is the product of an accidental kiss (literally a collision in a hallway). This conflation of personal weakness, blind chance, and simple clumsiness drives the sentimental narrative and produces significant anxiety among characters that already seem uncomfortable in fluid roles. Bellingham laments the fact that life is not as "well regulated" as "novels" (302) and agrees with Corey and Sewell that Barker would be better off if the sickly Statira would simply die. Her death would allow Barker to stay in Boston and find a woman who could "help him" into society. Sewell summarizes the complicated situation: " . . . [Barker] will still have an invalid woman on his hands; he must provide [Statira] a home; she could have helped him once, and would have done so I've no doubt; but now she must be taken care of" (302). It is chance that brings them together and "probability and human nature" that ultimately keeps them from marrying (312).

The relationship produces novelistic responses from the characters but has no effect whatsoever on the narrative. Howells capably manipulates his commentary on the novel within the novel here. Sewell spends much of the text trying to imagine a place for Barker in Boston and agonizing about the relationship with Statira; he uses both as the imaginative keys to his final sermon on "the care of others." Ultimately, however, his conclusions are empty and useless. Not only do they have a regrettable "novelistic" effect on his audiences, but also they prove inaccurate when Barker does not marry Statira and avoids the burden of her care. That Sewell reacts to the news with "a radiant smile of relief" underscores the wide disjunction between his ministerial words and his heart.

The Minister's Charge succeeds as a realistic novel precisely because it exposes this disjunction and allows the sermons, the courtship, and the surrounding narrative to be broadsided by the "deeper game" of "probability and human nature." For Howells, this success was precisely the source of his troubles; when he abandoned himself to the representational power of the novel and liberated his subjects, he found morality ("the novelist's grave duty to his reader") upstaged by blind chance. As Trachtenberg has observed, Howells wanted novel reading to be a serious exercise of civic faculties, a duty of no small consequence to the Republic.[18] Sewell would have his sermons produce the same effect, but like Howells he finds his ministry corrupted by his and his audience's reified class interests and self-conceptions. Although Howells could imagine a democratic middle ground—a space inhabitable by Coreys, Sewells, and Barkers—this space exists in *The Minister's Charge* only in the bewildered ideals of the poor and the insincere professions of the elite.

The human heart is the only democratic space in Howells's novels of the 80s, but it is radically out of step with intellect and ambition. Trachtenberg, Cady, Lynn, and Daugherty, among others, have worked to demonstrate that Howells practiced, or imagined himself practicing, a "restorative realism," a poetics of corrective vision that could strip from the democratic subject the layers of class-based expectations obstructing his or her perceptions of others. Sewell would serve this function within *Lapham,* attempting "to interpret Lapham to the Coreys as the novel itself attempts to interpret the entire Corey-Lapham world and all its misunderstandings, small and large."[19] In *The Minister's Charge* this neat formula collapses with Sewell's inability to interpret Barker's Boston experiences to anyone, least of all to himself.

Insofar as Sewell can be read as a fictional agent of Howells's hopes for a didactic fiction, he has the same difficulties as Howells negotiating the gap between private and public morality. John Seeyle argues that Howells has great difficulty locating a morality that he can apply simultaneously to self-cultivation, public duty, and literary calling: "Where Howells was willing to argue that self-sacrifice is wrong in affairs of the heart, being equated with sentimentality, he convinces us that in matters of social and business arrangements it seems to be still a fictive necessity."[20] As John Crowley points out, many critics have privileged Sewell as a character with a great deal of authorial weight behind him.[21] Some, like Michael Anesko, have gone so far as to raise his ministerial occupation with the subject of "complicity" to the level of Howells's guiding imaginative principle in the late eighties and early nineties.[22]

Such critical attention to Sewell seems misguided. While it is his act of false flattery that brings Barker to the city, the "rise" of Lemuel Barker has nothing to do with Sewell's words or acts. That Barker becomes an imaginative catalyst for Sewell's sermons and private meditations is entirely irrelevant to the former's rather rapid "citification." While Barker is a Bostonian—an inhabitant of the city, its public spaces, and marginally its social circles—he begins to realize as the narrative progresses that he is a Bostonian only when his mind is freed from anxieties about social station and prejudice. He does not, as Silas Lapham did before him, have the significations of "gross and palpable" wealth around him to give him a ready-made if imperfect class identity. He is a creature of the mind merely; a subject formed by observation and impression rather than object. This is the case for both of the primary voices in the text: Sewell and Barker exist outside of the tyranny of Gilded Age materialism, and yet they are caught indelibly inside of Boston's tense competing class ideologies—the sleight of hand of the Boston Common confidence men and the sleight of hand of the genteel aristocracy's claims to entitlement.

A text that results the clutter of material significations on both the thematic and formal levels, *The Minister's Charge* is driven by and devoted to an exploration of the effect of discourse on perception and ultimately self-actualization. Howells's resistance to the realist's tendency to emulate material culture in prose description reaches its zenith in *The Minister's Charge*. The text is utterly dialogue-driven, (enough to incite complaint from James, who had a vested interest in the sanctity of descriptive verbosity) and not yet given to the complex narrative observations so plentiful in *April Hopes*. The descriptions deploy material imagery frugally:

> There were more images in the garden that Barker came to presently: an image of Washington on horseback, and some orator speaking, with his hand up, and on top of a monument a kind of Turk holding up a man that looked sick. The man was almost naked, but he was not so bad as the woman in the granite basin; it seemed to Barker that it ought not be allowed there. A great many people of all kinds were passing through the garden, and after some hesitation he went in too, and walked over the bridge that crossed the pond in the middle of the garden, where there were rowboats and boats with images of swans on them. Barker made a sarcastic reflection that Boston seemed to be a great place for images, and passed rather hurriedly through the garden to the other side of the bridge . . . (29)

Barker's reception of the garden imagery is as innocent as it is suspicious; he is unsure whether this is the "Public Garden" and is not confident that he should have access to the images. This passage, as most in *Charge*, is virtually free of adjectives or other descriptive modifiers. Only the flowery novelistic language of the women boarders at the hotel deviate from this pattern. Barker cannot modify because he has no moral or aesthetic vocabulary with which to do so; Sewell cannot modify because of his ministerial iconoclasm. The

Boston aristocracy adopts the "colorful, ennobling" terms of novels, and the tramps in the park use their fast cadence and heavy dialect for grift.

It is on the aesthetic ignorance—even the moral illiteracy—of the highly average Barker that the narrative places the most value. He is educable, and as such he is a test subject for Howellsian realism. In this light, the change of the novel's title from varieties of "Lemuel Barker" to *The Minister's Charge or the Apprenticeship of Lemuel Barker* is most interesting. Howells and his publishers enacted the change at the earliest stages of serialization, at the same point that the text's attention shifts decisively away from Barker and toward Sewell's sometimes insipid self-doubts. The act of subordinating Lemuel would certainly have served to deflect some of the ceaseless criticism over Howells's "heroicizing of the common," and may accordingly have been a marketing maneuver. He had written with great frustration to James in December of 1886:

> If we regard [*The Minister's Charge*] as nothing but an example of work in the new way—the performance of a man who won't and can't keep doing what's been done already—its reception here by most of the reviewers is extremely discouraging. Of all grounds in the world they take the genteel ground, and every "Half-bred rogue that groomed his mother's cow," reproaches me for introducing him to low company. This has been the tone of "society" about it; in the newspapers it hardly stops short of personal defamation. Of course they entirely miss the very simple purpose of the book . . . [23]

"The simple purpose of the book," unidentified in this letter and elsewhere except as "an example of work in the new way" evaded James's careful eye as much as it evaded the contemporary critics. It almost certainly evaded Howells too, whose experimental "country boy" drops out of Boston and the narrative as quickly and surely as he stumbled in.

In the early stages of serialization, James had praised the developing "Barker" as "very triumphant" and later as "wholly perfect—better than anything yet—even than Bartley and Silas." He based his high estimation on the character 'Manda Grier, who was, he claimed, "so fine that I felt, as I went, as if I were writing her."[24] 'Manda, who speaks with thicker dialect than Barker and Statira, but not so thick as the Boston Common tramps and prostitutes, rarely stops talking. She is a character created by, driven by, and represented through ceaseless chatter, words that ultimately have greater effects on Lemuel and Statira than Sewell's sermons. Her parlor games, romantic notions, and empty rhetoric deny Lemuel and Statira the chance to speak but also frees them from the responsibility of speech: "Well, don't talk too much when I'm gone," said 'Manda Grier . . . Lemuel did not know what to do. The thought of being alone with Statira again was full of rapture and terror. He was glad when she seized the door, and tried to keep 'Manda Grier" (112). It seems likely that Howells, a man with a penchant for coded character names, chose "Lemuel" for Barker because of its proximity to the French *le muet,* "the mute."

It also seems hardly accidental that James would have been drawn to the most verbose and bombastic figure. 'Manda Grier and Sewell are creatures of spoken rhetoric and the power that its careful deployment can bring. Howells, well known for his discomfort as a public speaker, but simultaneously heavily invested in the transformative power of rhetoric, places Lemuel in the center of a swirl of competing persuasive ideologies.

It is through Lemuel, a figure free of class significations, that Howells enacts his first and most wide-ranging exploration of his own conflicted social and aesthetic personas. *The Minister's Charge* is not by any means an attempt by its author to eliminate his incoherence; rather, it is the first moment of Howells acknowledgement of his multi-vectored life and projects. As its title suggests, *The Minister's Charge* works to resolve the authorial urge to didacticism through an acceptance of the wide-ranging and even slippery significations of American youth. It is a text that equates innocence with confusion and therefore identifies didacticism—even the imposition of perceptual vocabularies through class, religion, or literary authority—as a necessary evil. The text's subplot is a record of useless bombast: its primary narrative is an appeal to moral and literary authority in an American culture too often defined and guided by the significations of bourgeois culture.

Chapter Two

A Hazard of New Fortunes and the "Aesthetic Immaturity" of the American Reader

> There is a difference between boys and men, but it is a difference of self-knowledge chiefly.
>
> — Howells, *A Boy's Town*

A year before the serial publication of *A Hazard of New Fortunes* in *Harper's Weekly* (March 23 through November 16, 1889), Howells responded to the enthusiastic national reception of Bellamy's *Looking Backward* with skepticism:

> [The book's] success . . . may well give pause to the doctor of literary laws, and set him carefully revising his most cherished opinions. For here is a book in which the sugar-coated form of a dream has exhibited a dose of undiluted socialism, and which has been gulped by some of the most vigilant opponents of that theory without a suspicion of the poison they were taking into their systems.[1]

His own realistic program widely ridiculed by the popular press and his cultural authority undermined by his recent public support of the Haymarket anarchists, Howells's cynicism was not aimed at Bellamy but rather at an American readership whose literary palate seemed to him increasingly unrefined. That the relatively forthright didacticism and utopian visions of *Looking Backward* had penetrated a national imagination so resistant to studies of contemporary American life like *The Minister's Charge* and *Annie Kilburn* further degraded Howells's sense of his own aesthetic potency.

"I'm not in a very good humor with 'America' myself," he wrote to Henry James in September, 1888, "It seems to me the most grotesquely illogical thing under the sun; and I suppose I love it less because it won't let me love it more."[2] Howells's cynicism reflects on one side his deepening sense of sympathy with the powerless and disenfranchised, a frustration with the corruptions of capitalism enflamed by his recent and passionate exposure to Tolstoy's radical Christianity. On the other side it suggests his very private feelings of betrayal, his notion that 'America'—or more precisely his potential readership—would not accept a literature dedicated to the day-to-day construction of the moral life of the democratic individual.

This image of "love" not reciprocated, this use of terms of affection to describe the relationship between Howells and his public, only grows stronger in Howells's writings through the late 1880s and into the 90s. Rooted at least in part in his childhood exposure to Swedenborgian notions of charity, devotion to "neighbor," and ideals of social formation and reformation, Howells's expressions of the individual's responsibility for his or her own salvation often directly contradict his sympathetic gestures to a voiceless American proletariat. It is not enough to broadcast messages of reform from a position of social or cultural power; such messages must be received, welcomed, processed, understood, and finally, acted upon. It is through this Swedenborgian conception of spiritual self-determination based on each thought and deed that Howells's complicated sense of audience can best be understood.

The clearest articulation of this author-reader relationship appears in an unexpected place, Howells's first earnest effort at autobiography: his 1890 *A Boy's Town* (published in *Harper's Young People* in that same year). It is the image of the "kindly earth-spirit," (or his closest boyhood friend, John Rorick) whose "soft, caressing ignorance" gave the young Will Howells some rest from his own "intensity of purpose," that captures this same intriguing combination of deep affection and disabling frustration.[3] The narrative voice of *A Boy's Town* suggests that young Howells felt an irrepressible desire—in fact a duty—to "elevate" and educate his truant friend. His efforts, however, led to humiliation for his friend, a degree of personal shame, and ultimately the utter disintegration of their friendship:

> [My boy] could not give him up, but he could not help seeing that he was ignorant and idle, and in a fatal hour he resolved to reform him. I am not able now to say just how he worked his friend up to the point of coming to school, and of washing his hands and feet and face . . . But one day he came, and my boy, as he had planned, took him into his seat, and owned his friendship with him before the whole school . . . He struggled through one day, and maybe another; but it was a failure from the first moment . . . The attempted reform had spoiled their simple and harmless intimacy.[4]

The language the narrator uses to describe this disintegration is interesting: the friends never met again "upon the old ground of perfect trust and affection" (193).

"Trust" and "affection" were also, at least for a time, the casualties of Howells's relationship with his reading public following the Haymarket affair and the journalistic backlash to his letter of protest. His uncertainties in these years extended beyond his sense of betrayal to a self-loathing reinforced by his textual emphasis on powerlessness and hypocrisy:

> I should hardly like to trust pen and ink with all the audacity of my social ideas; but after fifty years of optimistic content with "civilization" and its ability to come out all right in the end, I now abhor it, and feel that it is coming out all wrong in the end, unless it bases itself anew on a real equality. Meantime, I wear a fur-lined overcoat, and live in all the luxury money can buy.[5]

1888 marks a shift in Howells away from aesthetic, social, and personal activism. His language is characterized by a new passivity, a loss of confidence in and an increasing disgust with didacticism of any kind, from Bellamy's "sugar-coated forms" to the aggressive salesmanship of Howells's own pre-1886 exhortations for literary realism.

The shift of subject and theme between his 1888 *April Hopes* and 1889 *Annie Kilburn* demonstrates this personal and aesthetic movement: Howells began to abandon his often-repeated tropes of "new" money, "new" social blood, and the moral applications of wealth; the young Dan Mavering of *April Hopes,* son of wealthy wallpaper makers, stands as the last in a line of Howellsian social climbers. In *Annie Kilburn* these subjects find themselves reversed. Annie, returned to a Massachusetts mill town from a comfortable existence in the American colony in Rome, faces difficult questions of class separation, social union, and the response of the wealthy to unjust labor practices. It is at this juncture in Howells's aesthetic development that the Coreys and Bellinghams recede into the shadows, their voices of social censure and approbation silenced as surely as the foundering observations of Boston newcomers like Lemuel Barker and Silas Lapham. While this abandonment of trademark characters and novelistic formulae points first to Howells's frustration with the one audience on which he could reliably depend, his *Harper's* readers, it also marks an enrichment and complication of his fiction made possible by his abandonment of the didactic.

This shift in Howells's aesthetics has prompted some degree of debate among his critics. In *The Realism of William Dean Howells, 1889–1920,*

George Bennet argues against Cady's more broadly accepted suggestion that
Annie Kilburn is a "sugar-coated," soft, safe vehicle for ideas that might be unsavory to Howells's audience.[6] For Bennet, the divide between an intellectual
center (Peck) and an emotional center (Annie) in the novel, along with its resistance to "prescriptive and hortatory" presentations of economic and social
ideas, lends *Annie Kilburn* a complexity unknown in Howells's previous novels. In many ways the book is a study of the potency of art as an educative tool:
Annie's often frustrated desire to bring leisure and drama to factory girls, and,
toward the end of the novel, her "ironic awareness"[7] that she dwells in a "vicious circle . . . and mostly forgets, and is mostly happy" indicates Howells's
emotional complicity with her.[8]

Perhaps the clearest expression of Howells's loss of confidence in literary
activism is his rejection of William Morris's hopes for popular art and craft.[9]

> In one of his lectures ["The Aims of Art"], Mr. Morris asks his hearer to
> go through the streets of any city and consider the windows of the shops,
> how they are heaped with cheap and vulgar and tawdry and foolish gim-
> cracks, which men's lives have been worn out in making, and yet other
> men's lives in getting money to waste upon, and which are finally to be
> cast out of our houses and swept into our dust-bins . . . [10]

In this January 1890 "Editor's Study," Howells records Morris's vision of a future in which excellence of craft, not capitalistic competition, governs artistic
production. It is a vision that Howells himself rejects entirely—with an embittered tone—claiming that Morris fails to account for the "aesthetic immaturity" of the public: "those honest oxen, those amiable sheep, those worthy
donkeys . . . munch[ing] away at the grass . . ." desiring and consuming
"[m]ere fodder in all the arts." His use of such degrading and arguably classist
imagery coupled with his terms of affection ("honest," "amiable," "worthy")
recalls the "soft, caressing ignorance" of his childhood friend Rorick and that
earlier moment of despair at failed communication and education.

Howells wrote to his father in early 1890 that "it is a comfort to be right
theoretically, and to be ashamed of one's self practically."[11] This strange for-
mulation offers some insight into the peculiar trajectory of Howells's work
during his wanderings into and out of New York City between 1888 and
1891.[12] Much of his creative energy in these years emerged from a highly personal jeremiad: in his journals, letters to friends, and in the "Editor's Study"
column, Howells would repeat his case for a democratic literature that did not
"shelter itself in aesthetics."[13] Although he had for the most part by this point
abandoned "realism" as a usable and potent term, he continued to advocate

art that "wishes to know and to tell the truth, confident that consolation and delight are there."[14] While on the one hand he would celebrate a direct and accessible style, on the other he would berate an American public not "aesthetically mature" enough to digest his fiction. He would shelter himself in a cultivated class—whether on Beacon Street, Commonwealth Avenue, or in New York City—participating in the very process of class and aesthetic segregation that he would repeatedly condemn.

Only one month before his pivotal "Editor's Study" on the public's aesthetic immaturity, Howells's *A Hazard of New Fortunes* had been reviewed for its largest and most heterogeneous audience in the *New York Times*.[15] The review is decidedly positive in tone, announcing that "there is nothing lost of the vivacity that makes Mr. Howells's novels come like holidays among the novel-reading public." The reviewer takes a particular interest in Howells's "admirable discernment in the selection of his truth . . . while he is too sincere not too leave life as much at loose ends as he beholds it, he has trimmed his work close to the warp, and the connection and motive are maintained to the end." On the subject of "social questions," the reviewer comments only that they "are left necessarily unsolved; but the reader, still intellectually amused, is morally quickened." In short, the reader—like Annie Kilburn— leaves the social turbulence of the novel with a vague sense of *self* improvement but again "mostly forgets . . . and is mostly happy."

The "solubility" of social questions that this reviewer so easily dismisses is a subject of constant interest to Howells in the late 1880s. Thinking back upon this era in a 1909 introduction written for the Library Edition of *A Hazard of New Fortunes,* Howells remembers

> A period of strong emotioning in the direction of a humaner economics . . . the rich seemed not so much to despise the poor, the poor did not so helplessly repine. The solution of the riddle of the painful earth through the dreams of Henry George, through the dreams of Edward Bellamy, through the dreams of all the generous visionaries of the past, seemed not impossibly far off . . . Opportunely for me there was a great street-car strike in New York, and the story began to find its way to issues nobler and larger than those of the love affairs common to fiction . . .

It is hardly surprising that Howells remembers the period of composition of *Hazard* as a time of "emotioning" rather than action. In the above selection and elsewhere in this introduction he represents the composition of the novel with little reference to his own agency. "The story began to find its way" is one example of a tendency to remember *Hazard* as a text that wrote itself, that gained a creative independence from his control that he had never known before. It is an independence that he finds troubling: at the end of the piece he acknowledges that he finished the book very quickly—in a matter of months—while resting with his family in a rented house in Belmont, Massachusetts. Of this rapidity of production he says only "I had the misgiving which I always have of things which do not cost me great trouble."[16]

That Howells returns, in *A Hazard of New Fortunes,* to his two most familiar and admittedly autobiographical characters, Isabel and Basil March, suggests on the one hand a nostalgia for his earliest productions (*Their Wedding Journey,* 1872) and on the other a desire to address directly the maturation and transformation of his literary imagination. He writes: "When I began speaking of [these characters] as Basil and Isabel, in the fashion of *Their Wedding Journey,* they would not respond with the effect of early middle age which I desired in them . . . It was not until I addressed them as March and Mrs. March that they stirred under my hand with fresh impulse. . . ."[17] Howells's remembrances of his production of the novel are repeatedly characterized by a lack of control, a somewhat unpredictable process of self-reinvention and aesthetic reconceptualization.

Basil March, insomuch as he can be read as a partial and refracted representation of the authorial presence, speaks to this painful process of transformation. It is first evident in his family's unwillingness to accept the move to New York. His response is, at first, entirely conciliatory and accommodating to them. His *idea* of a new life, a transformed career and sense of self, remains secondary to the realities of his quotidian existence, and any expression of frustration or assertion of his own desires takes ironic or self-deprecating form. "I *was* dazzled by Fulkerson's offer, I'll own that; but his choice of me as editor sapped my confidence in him" (22).[18] His initial decision to reject the offer in reaction to Isabel's fears and his children's selfish complaints—"I've had an offer to go to New York, but I've refused it" (22)—is marked by an irony that falls "harmless from the children's preoccupation with their own affairs."

In a book populated by such a large number of strong-willed characters, many of whom are confident in their well-developed if not well-rounded world-views, Basil March stands in a peculiar isolation. His vision is marked by a lack of confidence, an observational innocence unwilling (or unable) to bring pre-established significations to his understanding of situations, scenes, individuals, and objects. The novel's narrator describes March's unfettered intellect affectionately, with an almost tender—and certainly a deeply personal—investment:

> [March] went to his business, and hurried back to forget it, and dream his dream of intellectual achievement . . . he could not conceal from himself

that his divided life was somewhat like Charles Lamb's, and there were times when, as he had expressed to Fulkerson, he believed that its division was favorable to the freshness of his interest in literature . . . He was proud of reading critically, and he kept in the current of literary interests and controversies. It all seemed to him, and to his wife at second-hand, very meritorious; he could not help contrasting his life and its inner elegance with that of other men who had no such resources. He thought that he was not arrogant about it, because he did full justice to the good qualities of those other people; he congratulated himself upon the democratic instincts which enabled him to do this . . . (26)

March appears here to be characterized by an aesthetic maturity that is a great source of pride to him. It is at once a literary-critical sensibility and a valuable life-skill. He is, in short, a fine reader of books and of human beings, and this skill emerges not primarily from education or station but rather from an energetic exchange between "business" and "intellectual achievement." In this passage, Howells's narrator constructs a vision of an idealized *reader,* one whose aesthetic sensibility permits a dialogue between literature and life.

It is difficult to argue that March is, however, the representative of the "mass of common men" that Howells calls on in *Criticism and Fiction* "to apply their own simplicity, naturalness, and honesty to the appreciation of the beautiful."[19] His sensibility, while self-consciously "democratic" is also smugly elitist. March is at once Howells's democratic man and a member of that "bad species . . . the false lights of critical vanity and self-righteousness."[20] As he and Mrs. March conduct their search for an appropriate New York City flat, they engage in a series of perceptual indulgences, a kind of highly self-conscious tourism:

They had crossed Broadway, and were walking over to Washington Square, in the region of which they now hoped to place themselves . . . they met Italian faces, French faces, Spanish faces, as they strolled over the asphalt walks, under the thinning shadows of the autumn-stricken sycamores. They met the familiar picturesque raggedness of Southern Europe with the old kindly illusion that somehow it existed for their appreciation, and that it found adequate compensation for poverty in this. March thought he sufficiently expressed his tacit sympathy in sitting down on one of the iron benches with his wife and letting a little Neapolitan put a superfluous shine on his boots, while their desultory comment wandered with equal esteem to the old fashioned American respectability which keeps the north side of the square in vast mansions of red brick, and the international shabbiness which has invaded the southern border, and broken it up into lodging-houses, shops, beer-gardens, and studios. (60)

March and his wife exhibit no carefully considered response to the complex of class and culture that they encounter near Washington Square. Their "desultory comment" suggests a certain automatic passivity: a half-hearted, "tacit" charity to the poor coupled with a clear sense of their own real or desired link to that "old American respectability." They imagine themselves as somehow separate from the "mass of common men," but are threatened by uncertainty as they wander "homeless" through New York. Their lack of property destabilizes their sense of self, and they must engage in class theatrics with each other and "poorer" New Yorkers to reinforce their imagined status.

"They came to excel in the sad knowledge of the line at which respectability distinguishes itself from shabbiness" (63). In the lengthy house-hunting section of *A Hazard of New Fortunes,* Howells experiments with the temporary removal of the middle-class American from his or her field of easy significations. Without property—specifically without a home—the Marches find themselves in a state of nervous self-evaluation. Basil and Isabel do not react in the same manner: Basil, characterized by his relative openness, "was still sunk in the superstition that you can live anywhere you like in New York," while his wife "found that there was an east and west line beyond which they could not go if they wished to keep their self-respect" (64). The gender dynamics in this scene—and indeed throughout *Hazard*—demonstrate the rift between Howells's imagined or ideal readership and his actual audience.

It is a subject he addresses with irony in *Annie Kilburn;* Annie's somewhat naïve attempts at social reform through art are endlessly mitigated by her emotional life. She lacks an intellectual center strong enough to articulate and enact her ideals. In *Hazard,* Mrs. March displays an unmistakable confidence and emotional force that regularly redirect her husband's less centered persona. While it is Basil that seems to maintain the more critical sensibility, it is Isabel that defines his subjects of critique. She is the concrete to his abstract, and as such, she holds a power inaccessible to him. Toward the end of the house-hunting section of the novel, March engages in a long reflection on the social and cultural effects of tenement life:

> 'Why, those tenements are better and humaner than those flats! There the whole family lives in the kitchen, and has its consciousness of being; but the flat abolishes the family consciousness. It's confinement without coziness; it's cluttered without being snug. You couldn't keep a self-respecting

cat in a flat; you couldn't go down to the cellar to get cider. No: the Anglo-Saxon home, as we know it in the Anglo-Saxon house, is simply impossible in the Franco-American flat, not because it's humble, but because it's false . . . '

'Well, then," said Mrs. March, "let's look at houses.'

He had been denouncing the flat in the abstract, and he had not expected this concrete result. But he said, 'We will look at houses, then.' (74)

Isabel's tacit practicality silences March; her punctuation of his developing ideas suggests Howells's own undeniable dependency on and frustration with his majority female readership. Unlike *A Boy's Town,* in which Howells represented the author-reader relationship through "his boy" and Rorick, here in *Hazard* he sets different styles of reading into competition. As the husband and wife "read" the visions of New York life that pass before them, Isabel works steadily to define her observations in terms of her immediate needs. Her requirements drive the action and her tastes determine decisions; Basil responds to her with compliance and affection, but his observations of the city and meditations on its complex life are undeniably curtailed by Isabel's demands. Their exchanges simultaneously illustrate and contain Howells's anxious awareness of the power that novel-reading American women have over his range of creation and expression.

His sense that he had a following limited to what one reviewer would call "fibrous virgins, fat matrons, and oleaginous clergymen" made the possibilities of New York City all the more intriguing to Howells. [21] He wrote to James that he hoped the "vast, gay, shapeless life" of the city would be of some use in his fiction.[22] The "use" he imagined involved at least in part separating himself imaginatively from the Boston landscape that had become over-familiar to him and too weighed down with personal significance for his largely New England readership. As he sought new venues for his imaginative work, his rhetoric toward the American reader changed sharply. In part a reaction to criticisms of *Annie Kilburn,* a novel called "unprofitable" by *The Nation,* "wearisome" by *The Critic,* and "tiresome" by *The Literary World,* Howells found himself caught between the desire to reinvent himself and the overwhelming sense that American critics—the arbiters of taste on whom he depended—had done him a severe injustice.[23]

One of Howells's first salvos against the aesthetic immaturity of the American reader appears in the September 1890 "Editor's Study." He writes with detectable anger about the reader who must have "the problem of a novel solved for him by a marriage or a murder, who must be spoon-victualled with a moral minced small and then thinned with milk and water, and familiarly flavored with sentimentality or religiosity."[24] The image here again is that of a child, one whose tastes are undeveloped and one who depends on some authority for guidance. It is the reader with no sense of self-reliance that Howells's angrily criticizes, but it is also the reader who accepts literature only when it gives pleasure. Howells argues through the "Study" for a mature understanding of the responsibility that comes with reading, an understanding that reading is a vital part of participation in a democratic process, that it is a form of engagement with life outside of the domicile.

In this sense, Isabel March is a spokesperson for the *worst* kind of reading. She is stirred only by extremes, and while she pleads with her husband that he not "sentimentalize any of the things [he] sees in New York," she does so because she doesn't believe "there's any *real* suffering—not real *suffering*—among those people; that is, it would be suffering from our point of view, but they've been used to it all their lives, and they don't feel their discomfort so much" (76). Isabel's consciousness is highly compartmentalized: her understanding of the universe is carefully mapped with lines, divisions, and borders. To "sentimentalize" for her is to feel complicity with the poor, a complicity she is unable to feel until she and Basil are directly confronted with a French beggar on the streets. Her response to his desperation is a demand to her husband that "we must change the conditions" of society to eliminate such suffering. The spontaneity and isolation of her remark, and the speed with which she is able to recover her good mood—suggest the substance of Howells's critique.

Although Isabel's quick and strong-minded responses to the unfamiliar social landscape of New York appear at first to represent an anti-Howellsian self-reflexivity, she does speak and act in the novel with a confidence unavailable to her husband. Basil, who exemplifies "the lenient, generous, and liberal life" so precious to the Howells of the 1880s, also exhibits the confusion and naiveté of a "realist" in a world governed by chance. In a competitive world where men and women must go "pushing and pulling, climbing and crawling, thrusting aside and trampling underfoot," Basil's "inner elegance" and "democratic instincts" fail him. While his wife reads New York confidently because of her unwillingness to accept the alienating and defamiliarizing face of her experience, Basil constantly sees in his environment a reflection of his own flawed character.

"The American," Howells wrote in *Criticism and Fiction*, "no more than any other man, shall know himself from his environment, but he shall know his environment from himself."[25] It is Isabel March who defines—or pretends to define—herself by her carefully triangulated social position, a position concretized by the property surrounding her. Basil March strives to "know his environment from himself" or more precisely to understand the ways in which his individual agency affects the conditions of his world, his country, and his city streets.

After his first encounter with Lindau, Basil reacts to his radical friend's "tasteless rhetoric" with benign disapproval:

> He could not doubt Lindau's sincerity, and he wondered how he came to that way of thinking. From his experience of himself he accounted for a prevailing literary quality in it; he decided it to be from Lindau's reading and feeling rather than his reflection. That was the notion he formed of some things he had met with in Ruskin to much the same effect; he regarded them as the chimeras of a rhetorician run away with by his phrases . . . (223)

The fanaticism of Lindau—"so fervent a hater of millionaires"—strikes Basil as ineffectual precisely because of its inelegance: such radicalism cannot translate into productive social change because it cannot manifest itself without violence. It is also profoundly *unpatriotic,* incompatible with the "democratic sensibility" that for Basil March is indelibly tied to a profound pride in one's American identity: " ' . . . I don't believe there's an American living that could look at that arm of yours and not wish to lend you a hand for the one you gave us all.' March felt this to be a fine turn, and his voice trembled slightly in saying it" (221).

The trembling in March's voice—perhaps a symptom of the same "sentimentalizing" tendency that his wife fears in him—betrays an optimism that forms the ironic center of *A Hazard of New Fortunes.* March's "aesthetic maturity" finds its clearest expression on the one hand in his unwillingness to give in to reckless radicalism and on the other hand in his refusal of the hubris characteristic of the American cultural and economic elite. What is left is a cautious and considered patriotism, a faith in a set of liberal American ideals that refuses to admit "chance" into its vocabulary. March's "optimism" *is* his naïveté, and the narrator of *Hazard* explores the ironic ineffectuality of this optimism with an embittered tone:

> He was interested in . . . the vagaries of the lines that narrowed together or stretched apart according to the width of the avenue, but always in wanton disregard of the life that dwelt, and bought and sold, and rejoiced or sorrowed, and clattered or crawled, around, below, above . . . [these] were features of the frantic panorama that perpetually touched his sense of humor and moved his sympathy . . . The whole at moments seemed to him lawless, godless; the absence of intelligent, comprehensive

> purpose in the huge disorder, and the violent struggle to subordinate the
> result to the greater good, penetrated with its dumb appeal to the con-
> sciousness of a man who had always been too self-enwrapped to perceive
> the chaos to which the individual selfishness must always lead . . . But
> there was still nothing definite, nothing better than vague discomfort,
> however poignant, in his half-recognition of such facts . . . (211)

March's over-aestheticization of such scenes, his tendency to turn his thoughts
to the "Dickensy" quality or at the very least to the literary applications of experience, points to his intellectual over-saturation. His optimism lies in his
ability to subordinate his "half-recognition" of social chaos to his fully developed artistic sensibility. This passage dramatizes the conflict within March:
his excellence as a reader of experience and his willingness to take observational risks are casualties of his sense of detachment from the "scenes" he studies. Rather than imagining himself as a functioning member of the American
polity, he becomes a sociologist, an anthropologist, and at his worst, a sentimental reader.

Basil refuses to admit his own detachment; it is a quality he detects and
identifies readily in Fulkerson's contempt for the magazine-reading public and
faith in advertising as the highest expression of the American mind. March,
confident that "the public will prove [Fulkerson] wrong," self-consciously
proceeds with his assembly of literary entries for *Every Other Week,* understanding fully that the magazine's sales are driven by color, art, and originally,
censure. His editorial position on the magazine's staff, his professional life, is
not the locus of his intellectual achievement. In fact, he has no satisfactory
medium for the expression of his aesthetic energies; they emerge, therefore, in
his daily walks and reveries, allowed no *professional* arena by the dollar-driven
world of publishing.

The novel takes no detectable stand on March's misapplication of his
well-developed democratic sensibility. Edwin Cady has argued that the novel
is "an investigation of the state of the American dream . . . conducted by Basil
March in the center with Lindau and Jacob Dryfoos as the polar opposites."[26]
George Bennet has expanded on Cady's reading by suggesting that the results
of this investigation "are inconclusive with respect to the economic pressures
and what a man should do to change them. There is no equivocation about
the wrongness of Dryfoos's pursuit of money, or about the fanaticism of
Lindau. There is, on the other hand . . . only private satisfaction in Basil's
stand for principle."[27] If Bennet is correct in his assertion that "Howells's final
resort [in *Hazard* is] to a kind of helpless irony in which the inadequacies of
both individual actions and theoretical general solutions are revealed," then

Howells's own remembrances of "strong emotioning" toward "humaner economics" seem suspect. While Basil March does stand between the extremes of
Lindau and Dryfoos, he does not represent a helpless irony as much as he represents a "half-recognition." *A Hazard of New Fortunes* is an investigation of
the state of the American dream *and*—perhaps more crucially—of the
American dreamer. March's sensibility often returns to a kind of sluggish private satisfaction, but it does so after a number of jarring instances of defamil-
iarization. The study of Basil March is the study of the potential for gradual
emotional change and, by extension, the study of the potential for gradual
democratic change.

For these reasons, Howells constructs March as a sensitive and capable
reader with all of the self-righteousness and smugness that he would expect
from a middle-class American and all of the contradictions built into the
gilded-age liberal democrat.

No figure in *Hazard* appears to have less in common with Basil March
than Conrad Dryfoos. While the novel surrounds Conrad with an almost beatified language, it does so ironically:

> His ideals were of a virginal vagueness; faces, voices, gestures had filled
> his fancy at times, but almost passionately; and the sensation that he now
> indulged was a kind of worship, ardent, but reverent and exalted. The
> brutal experiences of the world make us forget that there are such natures
> in it, and that they seem to come up out of the lowly earth as well as
> down from the high heaven. In the heart of this man well on toward
> thirty there had never been left the stain of a base thought . . . (322)

The narrator's language forms and sustains a complicity with the reader (" . . .
the brutal experiences of the world make *us* forget that there are such natures
in it . . .") that isolates Conrad even farther from the shared experience of the
novel. He is almost a non-character, a hyper-sentimentalized force that has
nothing to do with the highly practical world Howells creates in *Hazard*.
Conrad's ideals, while certainly comparable to Howells's own in the late 80s
and early 90s, lead to a self-destruction that cannot even successfully pretend
to martyrdom. His "virginal vagueness" is static and unproductive in the
novel; his goodness seems absurd, perhaps best exemplified at the moment of
his death: "He was going to say to the policeman: 'Don't strike him! He's an
old soldier! You see he has no hand!'" (491). His defense of Lindau is both
inarticulate and pathetic.

Neither Conrad nor Lindau has an ironic sensibility and thus neither
is able to survive in Howells's New York City. Their deaths are emblematic of
Howells's rejection of their way of seeing and understanding American

democracy. The streetcar riot itself, ostensibly a moment of high action and dramatic tension in the novel, is repeatedly diminished in importance by the novel's narrator and by Isabel's and Basil's reaction to it. On the page following the death of Conrad and the wounding of Lindau, the narrator reminds the reader that "we are creatures of the moment; we live from one space to another; and only one interest at a time fills these" (493). Isabel has already translated the tragedy to the narrow scope of her private universe: "To her mind, March was the principle actor in the whole affair, and much more important in having seen it than those who had suffered in it. In fact, he had suffered incomparably" (493).

The narrative works to deconstruct the reader's own response to Conrad's death, to undermine his or her tendency to sentimentalize a single act of violence. It is a moment at which the text forces the reader's hand, opening a space for reflection into the various levels of complicity one might feel with the rioters, the police, Conrad, Lindau, and the "combany bresidents" which Lindau declaims as he is struck down.

The complexity of March's reaction to the riot again identifies Howells's attention to gradual deliberation and slow emotional change. March slowly articulates his response to the event through the final one-hundred pages of the novel, moving from a vexed sadness ("Oh, death doesn't look so bad . . . it's life that looks so in its presence" (494)) to a sense of the irrelevance of individual actions, lives, and deaths ("I don't know what it all means, Isabel, though I believe it means good" (564)). Basil's realization that he has no entirely sincere response to the deaths, that his response, as well as his wife's, is ultimately selfish and self-referential, stands as the narrative's meaningful climax. "It's give and take in the business world, Isabel; especially take. But as to being uneasy, I'm not, in the least. I've the spirit of a lion when it comes to such matters" (509). Basil recognizes his complicity with the corrupt system; he recognizes his dependence on material wealth; he recognizes that "conditions *make* character; and people are greedy and foolish, and wish to have and to shine, because having and shining are held up to them by civilization as the chief good of life" (508). He emerges as an utterly self-conscious consumer of and participant in a structure of corrupt ideologies.

March does not change in any significant way, but his enhanced sense of his own complicity gives him a new vocabulary with which he is able to read and articulate the ironies of middle-class life. After acknowledging that neither he nor his wife is capable of "living simply," he meditates on the rarity and even impossibility of meaningful change:

'Does anything from without change us?' [March] mused aloud. 'We're brought up to think so by the novelists, who really have the charge of

people's thinking, nowadays. But I doubt it, especially if the thing outside is some great event, something cataclysmal, like this tremendous sorrow of Dryfoos's.'

'Then what *is* it that changes us?' demanded his wife . . .

'Well, it won't do to say, the Holy Spirit indwelling. That would
sound like cant at this day. But the old fellows that used to say that had
some glimpses of the truth. They knew that it is the still, small voice that
the soul heeds, not the deafening blasts of doom. I suppose I should have
to say that we didn't change at all. We develop. There's the making of several characters in each of us; we *are* each several characters, and sometimes this character has the lead in us, and sometimes that . . . 564

Just as Howells rejects the aesthetic usability of melodrama and artifice,
March rejects the "deafening blasts of doom," "cataclysm," and personal
tragedy as agents of meaningful change in an individual human life.[28] This
surprisingly transparent passage offers a glimpse of the point at which March
and Howells overlap and inform one another. March analyzes the changeability of the middle-class mind (and soul) with the terms of the novel and the
theatre. The layers of "character" in each individual strengthen and weaken in
response to event, education, and conscience. Human nature, as figured here,
is at once based in a universal "soul" and utterly centerless: individuality
emerges from some vague potentiality that shapes and solidifies according to
its exposure to the "still small voices" of ideology, structures of feeling, and
cultural expectations.

March declares here Howells's surrender of his faith in the novel's capacity to effect *measurable* change. It is the resolution of a crucial paradox in
Howells's aesthetic: In order to affect an individual through literature, one
must elicit a strong emotional response, but such a maneuver violates the
most essential edicts of Howellsian realism. The cynical or "fatalistic" solution
presented by March equates writing with an act of faith, and accepts a model
of the reader as largely unconscious, receptive in some vague way to the "still
small voice" that may, given the correct conditions, effect some minute
change in the development of a life. March senses no change in himself or in
Dryfoos, only a "stunned and benumbed" forced self-examination.

While the final pages of *A Hazard of New Fortunes,* those just following
March's cynical declarations, have been repeatedly criticized by analysts and
reviewers of the novel for what appears to be an overly contrived effort at closure, they can best be understood as an ironic satiation of the reader's need for
"a sugar coating." The narrator, having just abandoned March and his understanding of "the economic chance world" to some fatalistic calculus, takes the
reader through a final summary review of the novel's characters, ending with

the image of Margaret Vance "in the dress of the sisterhood which she wore" expressing from her eyes "the peace that passeth understanding" (575). Isabel takes a moment to ask her husband a question about Conrad's final conversation with Margaret, and her husband responds with disinterest: "I don't know. I don't care . . . Well, we must trust that look of hers" (575). The tangle of events that March has witnessed, all somehow leading to his own personal success as owner and editor of the *Every Other Week,* defy human understanding. He accepts the apparent randomness and absurdity of life on the one hand and on the other closes with a defiant faith in an order "that passeth understanding." Howells mocks himself through March, revealing the self-conscious contrivances of his novelistic closure, his understanding of the reader's hunger for a comprehensible conclusion, and his own desire for a literature of meaning, effect, and direction.

The conclusion of *A Hazard of New Fortunes* stands at once as a lesson in reading—a counterpoint to "spoon-victual" narratives like Bellamy's—and as Howells's gesture of surrender to such narratives. March is indeed a capable reader of books, of his world, and of his quotidian experiences, but he is also "benumbed" by the complexities and apparent injustices that he encounters in New York, injustices which as often as not benefit him and his wife. The "beatified" look on Conrad's face, and that "peace which passeth understanding" on Margaret's face stand as the most memorable images at the end of *Hazard.* The triumph of idealism—of a kind of witless religiosity— emerges as the only alternative to active acceptance of the paradigms of gilded-age capitalism. In essence, the only way to escape the "economic chance world" of *A Hazard of New Fortunes* is to leave it: to enter a cloister or to die.

Such a reading does suggest that Howells had reached the deepest point of his own pessimism around 1890, but it is not an utterly deterministic vision.[29] March's ironic sensibility, his ability to stand at a distance and observe his own failings with the same attention he pays to Lindau's, Dryfoos's, or Beaton's exposes the transparency if not the changeability of the corrupt capitalistic system. *Hazard* is a novel about *seeing* and about *self-knowledge* more than it is a call to reform; it is a study of virtue as much as it is a study of corruption, an honest examination of the ways in which the defects of virtue can only contribute to the perpetuation of corruption.[30] By allowing March to call into question the easy binary opposition of "virtue" and "greed," Howells forces his reader to evaluate his or her own complicity with social evil.

It is a complicity Howells felt acutely in his own literary life and one that was exacerbated by his recently redefined pariah status among American writers and critics. That he was forced so quickly to move from a sense of himself as a bold inventor and avant-garde thinker to a "wearisome" old moralist alienated him from his own sense of authorship more than it alienated him from any specific readership. Howells was increasingly unsure of himself as an intellect in the late 80s and early 90s. More precisely, he doubted his own aesthetic maturity and his ability to mediate between complex economic ideas and the imaginative sphere of his novels. As Henry Steele Commager has argued, Howells never really understood the problems to which he addressed himself; he knew the middle classes, but he neither knew the world of the very rich nor the world of the very poor. "Nor was his gift that of broad interpretation or sweeping generalization; he was happy only with the minute, the particular, and the personal . . . when he tried to explain the failure of the competitive system, he became bogged down [in] pale abstractions."[31] In short, how could Howells expect "aesthetic maturity" from his imagined readership if he could not manage any more than a vague "emotioning" in his novels?

Just after the completion and publication of *A Hazard of New Fortunes,* an article by Edmund Gosse appeared in the American journal the *Forum* outlining "The Limits of Realism in Fiction."[32] Gosse pays only cursory attention to Howells in the article, the probable result of residual anger against the American for his "Editor's Study" invectives against English novelists. "The time has hardly come," writes Gosse, "when we look to America for symptoms of literary initiative" (400). Importantly, however, Gosse uses the article to identify what he sees as an essential limitation in the realistic novel, one Howells certainly intuitively identified and understood but never directly addressed. Referring specifically to texts by Henry James and Zola, Gosse writes:

> . . . built up as they are with infinite toil by two of the most accomplished architects of fiction now living, [such texts leave] on the mind a sense of strange reflection, of images blurred or malformed by a convexity of the mirror. As I have said, it is difficult to account for this, which is a feature of blight on almost every specimen of the experimental novel; but perhaps it can in a measure be accounted for by the inherent disproportion which exists between the small flat surface of a book and the vast arch of life which it undertakes to mirror, those studies being least liable to distortion which reflect the smallest section of life, and those in which ambitious masters endeavor to make us feel the mighty movements of populous cities and vast bodies of men being the most inevitably misshapen . . . (398)

Faced with a community of critics unsatisfied with his studies of the "smallest section of life" and frightened by the distortions of Jamesian romance and the unmanageable realities of the economic-chance world, Howells could only read Gosse with a sense of his own aesthetic over-reaching in *A Hazard of New Fortunes.*

Howells would increasingly recognize the incommensurability of his politics with his imaginative productions. Just as March had protested in principle against Dryfoos's mistreatment of Lindau, Howells had made a good show of his socialism in his support of the Haymarket "anarchists"; however, like March, he would never have to suffer or sacrifice for his principles in any measurable way. Similar to "his" child in *A Boy's Town,* Howells wields the pen capably but hesitates to engage in a meaningful confrontation.

In his 1982 essay on Balzac entitled "Realism and Desire," Fredric Jameson describes the complicated authorial presence (he calls it the *fantasm* or *fantasy* element) in the realistic novel. It is the imagined self, the projected fantasy of the self's place in family and history, Jameson suggests, that constitutes the authorial presence in a text that lays claims to realism. This formula seems well-suited to Howells, whose sense of cultural authority and national duty—"the truth he was born to proclaim"—was so radically divergent from his creative and deeply personal anxieties. Howells's polyvocal novels, and *A Hazard of New Fortunes* specifically, enact a narrative of national self-examination on class and an extended fantasy-reconciliation of his confident public persona with his irresolute private fears. In this sense Howells fractures himself into author, character, and reader; when he imagines his young self in *A Boy's Town,* when he projects a part of himself through March, when he criticizes his own readership in "The Editor's Study," he engages in a messy process of self exploration. While Gosse identifies the chief limitation of the realistic novel to be its inability to reflect the "vast arch of life," Howells counters with a vision of the novel not as mimetic but as introspective. By doing so he responds to his own criticism of the "aesthetic immaturity" of the American reader by acknowledging and representing the same phenomenon in himself.

Chapter Three

"Disintegrating under the Reader's Eye": The Aging Howells and His Public, 1890–1920

> . . . Every interest, as already said, attaches itself to an object. The artist is interested in his brushes, in his colors, in his technique. The business man is interested in the play of supply and demand, in the movement of markets, etc. Take whatever instance of interest we choose and we shall find that, if we cut out the factor of the object about which interest clusters, interest itself disappears, relapsing into mere subjective feeling . . .
>
> — John Dewey, "Interest in Relation to Training the Will," 1895

Writing for the *New York Tribune* on August 18, 1891, Stephen Crane recorded a portion of a lecture delivered by Hamlin Garland on William Dean Howells:

> . . . the test of the value of Mr. Howells's work will come fifty years from now, when his sheaf of novels will form the most accurate, sympathetic and artistic study of American Society yet made by an American. Howells is a many-sided man, a humorist of astonishing delicacy and imagination . . . He is by all odds the most American and vital of our literary men to-day. He stands for all that is progressive and humanitarian in our fiction, and his following increases each day. His success is very great, and it will last.[1]

Garland's generous assessment of Howells's career and Crane's reportage of it may have been transparently self-serving, but this lecture portion does provide strong evidence that Howells's status in American literary canons was not in doubt in 1891. The "test," at least to Garland, was to be the endurance of Howells's increasingly massive collection of works.

After over a century of critical and popular evaluations, we know that the results were not so grand. Howells, though recognizable in name to most students of American literature and culture, is almost entirely unread. This slip into obscurity is a visible process, especially after 1900, but it cannot be attributed to the infirmities of age. The period between the turn of the century and his death in 1920 was, quantitatively, Howells's most productive. In fact, his appointment as the author of the *Harper's* "Editor's Easy Chair" in 1899 involved a mandatory three thousand words per month over and above his numerous private projects in multiple genres. In total, Howells wrote forty-nine book-length texts in the twentieth century; some were rather brief farces or dramatic scenes, but most were novels or memoirs exceeding 150 pages. Upon his death he was in the middle of several projects, the most significant of which was probably his three-volume autobiography; only Part One, *Years of My Youth* (1916), reached completion.

It is the purpose of this chapter to explore the ways in which William Dean Howells responded imaginatively to his decreasing cultural relevance after 1900. Not merely a function of age, Howells's disenfranchisement represented a measurable shift in the American publishing industry toward promotion and marketing among a widening and increasingly dominant middle class. The transforming marketplace paralleled a new understanding of the materials and motives of "realistic fiction," and Howells found himself suddenly assuming a defensive posture after the turn of the century.

His late fiction provides a catalog of these new concerns. Always opportunistic and attentive to cultural change, Howells struggled to adapt to the emergent consumerism that began to dominate literary economics and aesthetics. His texts of the late 1890s to around 1905 contain the first glimmers of anxiety, most clearly visible in the revisions of Howells's most often-cited motif: the house. While houses appear throughout his body of imaginative texts, and there is no shortage of work on their complex significations, few have addressed the internalization and reconfiguration of Howells's house imagery that takes place in the twentieth century. The house becomes a place imperiled from the inside and out by "questionable shapes" in the night and by wandering tramps and thieves. It becomes a place of intergenerational and interclass conversation, rarely genial, always strained. Stable foundations are replaced by cabins, inns, and storage compartments. These same images populate Howells's "Editor's Easy Chair" column from 1900 through 1920 and appear in the context of his discussions of the literary marketplace. It is the phenomenon of the "publishing house," an institution through which Howells defines himself with increasing difficulty, that dominates his imagination after 1900.

For Howells, the book was an ordering force. His realism was indebted to and embedded in the rhetoric of transcendentalism. To read a Howellsian novel during the nineteenth century was, the author hoped, to see the order and goodness of American society beneath the increasingly messy material clutter of the age. The Howellsian realist "cannot look upon human life and declare this thing and that thing unworthy of notice, any more than the scientist can declare a fact of the material world beneath the dignity of his inquiry. He feels in every nerve the equality of things and the unity of men; his soul is exalted, not by vain shows and shadows and ideals, but by realities in which alone the truth lives."[2] Howells's aesthetic and pedagogical programs directly contradicted the lessons of consumer culture that opposed in every way "the equality of things and the unity of men."

In the early-twentieth century, this Emersonian brand of cultural reform, directed to a lettered elite with dwindling popular cache, seemed archaic if not absurd. Howells never stopped writing for the genteel upper and middle classes. He knew that these same groups bought and read the majority of the popular romances of the day, and he worked steadily to create a diversified body of realistic works (by him and by his colleagues and protégés) that could compete with the more "compelling genres."[3] Despite his unwillingness to reach out to a new audience, Howells had enough diplomatic savvy to understand the increasing age and decreasing influence of his readership. Even in the 1890s Howells was grappling with his increasing distance from the mainstream of public opinion and media interests: "I would not have the *young author* . . . believe that it is well either to court or to defy the good opinion of the press. In fact, it will not only be better taste, but it will be better business, for him to keep it altogether out of his mind" (emphasis mine).[4]

This advice for the young author, certainly directed outward toward such protégés as Crane, Garland, and Norris, was also self-referential: it was difficult for Howells to accept the distance between his own literary projects and the increasingly radical realism that he sanctioned in his reviews. Only a few years before, the very notion of literary realism had been received as a somewhat radical departure from 19th century romantic conventions. Now the radical had become the conservative almost overnight, and the turn-of-the-century enthusiasm for newness and intensity left Howells looking—and probably feeling—old beyond his years.

Beginning around 1900, Howells's publications received only polite consideration and lukewarm reviews, but despite this increasingly vexed reputation among his fellow artists and writers, Howells continued to receive generous offers from publishers. A 1897 letter from George Harrison Mifflin to Elizabeth Stuart Phelps demonstrates both an awareness of his value and an anxiety about his fading artistic relevance. Phelps had complained to Mifflin after hearing that Howells had received a higher royalty percentage than she. Mifflin responded to her:

> You speak of Howells getting for example 20 percent and being a "rolling stone." The first suggestion is I am sure a mistake, and I think Howells never made a more fatal false step than when he entered upon that failing rolling stone policy. His books now simply don't sell, and he finds doors once so hospitably open now closed to him. I may say to you in strictest confidence that we recently had the offer of bringing to-gether all his books for a final "definitive" Edition, which had it been made and sold by the methods we had in mind should have brought him in a permanent and steady income . . . but we declined the offer . . . and this because owing to his methods he has written himself out, and so scattered his works that he has killed the goose so to speak that "laid the golden egg" . . . [5]

The "method" and the "rolling stone policy" refer to Howells's contracts with multiple publishers during the 1890s. It was Mifflin's studied opinion that Howells's texts would never be marketed or advertised sufficiently because the author was too expensive. Merely acquiring a Howells text drained a pub-lisher's budget, and it is probably this fact that prevented Howells's works from being collected and published in a definitive, complete edition during his life. Even Harper & Brothers, Howells's primary publisher after 1899, never completed the task. J. Henry Harper notes his *intention* to do so in 1912: "We are just on the eve of publishing a complete Library Edition of the works of W. D. Howells."[6] This edition would never appear. Only much later, in the 1970s, would a collection of Howells's complete works emerge from the University of Indiana Press, driven more by nostalgia than marketability.

As Cady notes in *The Realist at War*, it seems to have been Howells's very eminence which robbed him of his best and truest monument. Although Duneka (of Harpers) had sent him a complete prospectus of the *Library Edition*, design was too be extremely elaborate and expensive, and the collec-tion was to comprise a total of forty volumes. Only six reached the market: *My Literary Passions & Criticism & Fiction; The Landlord at Lion's Head; Literature and Life; London Films & Certain Delightful English Towns; Literary Friends and Acquaintance;* and *A Hazard of New Fortunes.* Henry Rood, the chief designer of the collection, wrote that the project had been wrecked by disputes "concerning details of copyright and adjustment of financial mat-ters."[7] This failure to produce a single, collected, unified edition of all of his works left Howells's legacy scattered and disorganized. Only the most devoted readers would have a sense of the breadth of his career, and his decades of carefully composed essays, columns, editorials, and reviews would be consigned to the dusty pages of aging—and ephemeral—periodicals.

New England literary periodicals were undergoing their own rather sudden gentrification at the turn of the century. Increasingly stable financially but subject to a fickle public, many East Coast houses (among others, Houghton Mifflin, Harper & Brothers, Charles Scribner & sons, and later Harcourt, Brace, & Co.) became less loyal to and dependent on particular authors. Howells had a remarkable talent for what Edwin Cady called "dickering"; he was able to navigate the troubled waters of the marketplace with skill and measurable success.

By early 1892 Houghton Mifflin (successors to Ticknor) were paying Howells 20 percent on *A Modern Instance, A Woman's Reason, Indian Summer, The Rise of Silas Lapham,* and *The Minister's Charge* and $16^2/_3$ percent for plays and paperbacks. At this rate Howells was securing $2,000–$2,500 a year in royalties, a rate he significantly improved through a fresh deal with Harpers later in the year. Howells gave Harpers first consideration of books for five years, getting 20 percent of retail for the first 5,000 sales and 25 percent after. With this deal he also raised royalties to a flat 20 percent on *April Hopes, Annie Kilburn, A Hazard of New Fortunes, The Shadow of a Dream,* and *An Imperative Duty.*[8] Edwin Cady cites a March 31, 1893 notebook entry in which Howells records opportunities, responsibilities, and prospects equaling $29,400 through eight contracts with separate publishers. Not only is this an impressive number for the time, but it is also a testimony to Howells's remarkable skills as a negotiator and self-promoter.

Adept as a freelance writer, Howells's value continued to increase. He sold *My Literary Passions* to Edward Bok and the *Critic* for $10,000; Alden and *Harper's* were willing to bid $7,000 in 1899 to serialize *Their Silver Wedding Journey* and $10,000 for the never written *History of Venice.*[9] As Cady points out,

> His value to the magazines was unique. The dependability of his faithful audience was a sound asset. His enmity toward the sources of appeal to the big public market was a liability. It is also probable that his high magazine price and very high royalties—20 and 25 per cent on the retail price of a book—discouraged publishers from plunging on big advertising budgets for him. In the long run, Howells depended on keeping the value of his name high through the cumulative prestige of his total career. That, and his steady productiveness, preserved his marketability. His system denied him flashy commercial success. But it gave him security and

an excellent living together with freedom to do his own real work as his understood it.[10]

Ultimately, though, Howells's marketability would become less relevant as he would commit to an exclusive contract with the Harpers, one that was seen, by both parties, as providing a measure of security. Howells and the Harpers invested in each other.

1899 was a year of tremendous uncertainty for Harpers, as it was for a number of other publishing houses. The agreement with Howells, arranged by George Harvey, editor and owner of the *North American Review*, recently appointed "agent" (by J.P. Morgan), and president of Harpers after February 17, 1900, demonstrated the clear link between Howells's return to the firm and the Harpers' survival. Cady records the details of the deal:

> For $10,000 a year the Harpers were to take all Howells wrote. He was to revive the "Editor's Easy Chair," contribute occasional short stories to *Harper's Monthly*, articles to Harvey's *North American Review*, and serve the firm as literary counselor. In that last capacity he was to continue his natural work with young writers—but for the benefit of the firm if possible—and solicit manuscripts.[11]

This sizeable investment in Howells, more an executive appointment than a writer's contract, would stabilize his career but all but eliminate his flexibility. With so much invested in him, Harper's would be reluctant, as other houses had been before 1899, to spend much money advertising and marketing Howells. He was, for the house, a conservative and dependable investment, one that would allow Harpers to take risks with younger writers.

J. Henry Harper exuberantly acknowledges this continuing relationship with Howells in his 1912 *The House of Harper*, one of the first of a series of publishing histories and genealogies written in conjunction with the major houses after 1910:

> . . . Mr. Howells, who has so worthily earned his title of "Dean of American Letters," is a literary diamond of so many brilliant facets that it would be idle for me to attempt the slightest explication of his genius in the space or with the talents at my disposal. Renowned as a novelist, poet, critic, essayist, editor, and social reformer though he is, I think of him more often as a loyal and inspiring friend . . . ready to bring his serene counsel and unquestioned powers into play for the benefit of his associates. The task of presenting him with any degree of adequacy to the readers of these pages was so completely beyond me that I early abandoned the attempt . . . [12]

Harper's enthusiasm for Howells is an interesting twentieth-century inversion of the writer-patron relationship; here it is the financier who praises the venerable author, acknowledging the interdependency of literary reputation and business acumen in the changing marketplace.

Howells returns the favor to Harper only a few pages later in an excerpted portion of his letter to the author:

> . . . In business, which the ignorant think altogether sordid, many delicate and generous things are done . . . I have remained attached to the House of Harper & Brothers, with no desire for any other business relations. As there is some superstition to the contrary, and authors and publishers are supposed to be natural enemies, I think I may properly testify here to the friendship which has always existed between my publishers and myself . . . [13]

Here is Howells the "dickerer" engaged in the kinds of rhetoric he most enjoyed and most skillfully employed. He by no means eliminates the "suspicions" that surround his loyalty to the Harpers; in fact, in typical form Howells draws a subtle line between "business" and "friendship," keeping the former in doubt while ensuring the permanence of the latter. Harper seems to recognize the barb, and follows his excerpt from Howells's letter with a reminder of Howells's age: "Howells possesses a wonderful fund of humor and youthful vigor for a man who has passed his threescore years and ten."[14]

How unusual was Howells's relationship with his turn-of-the-century New England publisher? Comparing financial data among several houses from the years 1899–1915 puts Howells's contract into clear relief. He was almost always the exception rather than the rule; it seems clear that other houses would have envied the Harper's acquisition because it gave them a stable link to the hard-to-please "gentle readers" of the late 19th century while allowing them to expand, with an authoritative stance, into the new "poetic sunburst" that was radically reconfiguring the North American literary marketplace.

The *Atlantic Monthly*, the magazine that gave Howells his triumphant start in the 1860s and 1870s, provides an interesting case study for the larger market during these years.[15] In 1899, Bliss Perry became the newest member of the periodical's illustrious editorial genealogy. His colleague, MacGregor Jenkins, assumed the role of "promotion manager" for the magazine, a new position made necessary by the challenges of the expanding and transforming market. The question on any editor's or publisher's mind at the time was how to satisfy the "gentle readers" who had so long supported magazines like the *Atlantic Monthly* and *Harper's Monthly* while at the same time appealing to the vast, younger, and regionally diverse readership appearing in many American cities. This tension is beautifully illustrated by a story that Ellen Ballou records in her history of Houghton Mifflin, *The Building of the House*. Having received an unsolicited manuscript from Henry James in 1900, Bliss Perry could not resist the opportunity to publish it. After doing so, however, MacGregor Jenkins "besought [Perry], with actual tears in his eyes, not to print another story by James" since he was trying desperately to convince the reading public, and investors, that "the *Atlantic Monthly* was not a high-brow magazine."[16]

The image of Henry James's style bringing tears to a publisher's eyes appropriately illustrates the confused state of the publishing industry around 1900. Indeed, the *Atlantic Monthly* was in serious financial trouble. Houghton Mifflin suffered a $10,000 loss on the magazine in 1901, and did not make a profit again until a $2,000 gain in 1907—its fiftieth anniversary year. Even in this celebratory year, the *Atlantic* circulation was far outstripped by its primary competitor, the *World's Work*, which claimed a circulation of 100,000 to the *Atlantic's* 18–20,000.[17]

An almost accidental event in 1907 changed the fate of the *Atlantic Monthly* by restructuring the demographics of its subscribers. While Bliss Perry was briefly on sabbatical, his temporary replacement, future editor Ferris Greenslet, ran a section of *The Helpmate* by English writer May Sinclair. The text opens with a man and his wife in bed, surrounded by a messy room filled with randomly strewn clothes. Despite Greenslet's concerns, May Sinclair insisted that her story be serialized without any alterations. Greenslet agreed. The (perhaps unsurprising) result: scores of New England subscribers cancelled; however, to the shock and delight of the *Atlantic Monthly* and Houghton Mifflin, two subscribers from west of the Mississippi joined for every New Englander who left. The magazine's profits briefly soared, and May Sinclair earned a sizeable paycheck.[18]

It is worth noting, however, that even Sinclair's paycheck, $3,500 for a twelve-part serial (the highest on record from the *Atlantic*, 1900–1910), seems dwarfed by Howells's consistent rate of pay during the same period. Ballou records the following approximate rates of pay for some recognized authors from 1900–1909:

Bliss Perry's total monthly budget for the *Atlantic*	$1440
Atlantic's mean rate for articles	$10 per 700 words
	$8 for Contributors' Clubs
Henry James	$15 per page
Charles Eliot Norton	$20 per page
Jack London	$120 per piece (non-serialized short)
William Dean Howells[19]:	$350 per piece (non-serialized short)[20]

Again, Howells's value to his publishers endangered his legacy. Cady's assessment seems appropriate: "If [Howells] is to be criticized in this final period of his Deanship, it should be for pumping too hard at the wells, not for neglecting them."[21]

Regardless of the intensity of Howells's efforts, new copyright laws were directly impacting the bankbooks of his many publishers. The International Copyright Act of 1891, in particular, made literary advertising a viable and reliable tool for American publishers. As Daniel Borus explains, before the Act, literary "pirates" could undersell established firms and profit doubly from any advertising expenses a firm might accrue. By the turn of the century, however, legal protections liberated the publishers and inflated their advertising budgets to as high as $75,000 annually. The Act also allowed for the emergence of literary agents, who originated in America after the Copyright Act as contacts for British publishers.[22] Howells's relationship with literary agents, as an institution, was a mixed one: as a novelist and a dickerer he coveted the opportunity to squeeze more money out of publishers by means of the competitive marketplace. As an arbiter of taste and a reviewer of books, Howells felt significantly weakened by the increasing power individual writers gained through relationships with agents. Agents knew how to exploit "niche markets" and how to market writers as products designed for the needs of specific publishers. Popular taste increasingly drove editorial decisions, and Howells's controlling project was still, as it always had been, the exact opposite.

The marketplace did not, of course, reconstruct itself overnight. Significant conservative factions maintained their sway in New York and in Boston. In this sensitive transforming marketplace, a conservative investment in Howells was seen as significantly wiser than a series of high-risk ventures with untested experimentalists like Theodore Dreiser. The "venerable" periodicals hesitated even to touch many of the more radical emergent realists and naturalists. It was, in fact, the relatively new Doubleday and Page that accepted Dreiser's *Sister Carrie* manuscript for publication in the spring of 1900. The then editor and director of Doubleday and Page, Walter Hines Page, attempted to break the contract only a few months following its acceptance; he reportedly found the book's treatment of female sexuality and Dreiser's use of real names and real places unsavory and predicted a popular failure. The contract survived, and the first edition of *Sister Carrie* appeared in a very limited print run of 1,000. Only half of these sold. After this initial failure, *Sister Carrie* emerged, with the help of literary agents, into the market and into America's intellectual landcape with full force seven years later. B. W. Dodge and Co. reissued it in 1907 and sold 8,500 copies. It has remained in print since.[23]

The newest generation did not regard Howells with as much veneration as Garland had a decade before. Despite his debt to Howellsian realism, Dreiser saw himself as an inheritor and transformer of Howells's legacy rather than the next torchbearer.[24] Although he rejected the idea of literary patronage (Howells did not offer it; he told Dreiser that he "did not think much" of *Sister Carrie*) he presented himself to publishers as someone writing literature that was directly in touch with the American cultural moment. Amy Kaplan suggests that Dreiser constructs "an idealized world no longer available to Howells's generation—nor indeed to Howells—a world in which literature is integrated into other ways of life . . . in which writing is a pleasurable form of artisinal work, whose value lies in community service."[25] Rather than rejecting Howells's aesthetic program outright, Dreiser recognized its importance and influence not only in narrative fiction but also in poetry, the nonfiction of the muckrackers, and even in the simple and early narratives of the burgeoning American film industry.[26] Photojournalists like Jacob Riis (*How the Other Half Lives*) acknowledged their sympathy with Howells's projects as early as 1890. Dreiser and his generation were by no means as antagonistic to Howells as Brooks and Mencken would be ten to twenty years later precisely because the publishing industry was broadly and increasingly complicit with the marketing possibilities of "realistic" fiction. Howellsian realism, in Corkin's words, emphasized "visually available materials and an effort to join a notion of morality with the modern dictates of expedience." Although Corkin here mistakes the increasingly hegemonic perversions of Howells's aesthetic vision for the thing itself, he does appropriately identify the moment at which Howells the man began to drift away from his now independently animated projects. When "realism" began to speak to an increasingly dominant middle-class readership, it was a generation of newcomers, like Dreiser, who took the podium. Howells, who had always worked to broadcast his messages from the top of society, now found his audience increasingly insular and irrelevant.

Howells was not alone in his battle for relevance in the twentieth-century marketplace, but he was the most serious casualty. The narrator of Howells's *Imaginary Interviews* (1910) meditates on the status of the "veteran author" in the new century:

> . . . The misgiving was forced upon [Eugenio] by certain appearances in the work of other veteran authors. When he took up the last book of some lifelong favorite, no matter how great a master he knew him still to be, he could not help seeing that the poor old master was repeating himself, though he would not have phrased the case in such brutal terms . . . [27]

To the Harpers and to Scribner, the cultural "relevance" of Howells, Mark Twain and even Henry James had very little to do with their continued publication. As Daniel Borus points out, these three "veterans" belonged to the same broad category of consumption. They were well-established personalities whose texts provided valuable advertising space. The space used in various editions of their texts provides clues to the perceived value of their personalities in the broader market. The first edition of Howells's *Questionable Shapes* (1900) includes a lengthy advertising section plugging both Howells's other texts and works by Mrs. Humphrey Ward and Henry Seton Merriman. These sections become shorter as the century progresses. By 1910, Harpers abandons advertising in Howells's editions, and by 1916, in *Years of My Youth,* Harpers takes the space only to list "other autobiographical works by the same author."[28]

The disappearance of these advertising pieces may not have been solely the result of Howells's increasing cost and decreasing relevance; in fact, publishing houses were expanding their pool of marketing resources. "Author at home" books and articles became extremely popular around the turn of the century. Well-informed readers knew all there was to know about a veteran author's private life and habits (Howells's cigars and bear-skin coats, Twain's Tiffany decorations, James's English cottages). In short, each author's life became public property, and each neatly packaged "at home" text or article increased the public appetite for literary celebrity.[29] It was not the publisher's intention to market Twain, James, or Howells, but rather to establish and reinforce the performative dimension of authorship. A new book from a given publisher was to carry the same force as a new production from a celebrated theatre company: the newest actors would be given special attention and would draw sizable crowds.

Needless to say, "Howells at home" was significantly less interesting to the new middle-class readership than the increasingly eccentric Twain or the expatriate James. These two, both close friends of Howells until their deaths, had very different publishing experiences in the first decade of the twentieth century, and it is interesting to note that despite their close associations, the three very rarely discussed their rates of pay or the breadth of their readership. James and Twain remained reasonably comfortable and secure in the first decade of the twentieth century, although the panic year of 1907—the same year that saw the triumphant emergence of *Sister Carrie*—forced them to take 10 percent pay cuts.

Twain, like Howells, gave Harvey of Harpers a promise for exclusive rights to all future works in 1900. He wrote in a 1903 notebook entry that the contract "concentrates all my books in Harper's hands and now at last they are valuable: In fact they are a fortune. [Harper's] guarantee me $25,000 a year for five years, and they will yield twice as much . . . if properly handled."[30] By November, 1914, $314,300 had been paid to Twain and his heirs by the Harpers—a fortune indeed.[31] Perhaps more interesting than the numbers themselves, Harvey proposed on October 17, 1900 that Twain's memoirs, along with one hundred autographed sheets, be kept under seal by a trust company until the year 2000, when Harper's would issue them "in whatever modes should then be prevalent, that is by printing as at present, or by use of phonographic cylinders, or by electric methods, or by any other method which may then be in use." This kind of forethought underscores the breadth of commitment that the Harpers were willing to make to Twain, a figure who represented for them compounded profit, profit that they forecasted into the 21st century. Their prediction proved correct, and it stands to reason that the significant marketing efforts surrounding Twain cemented his place in the American canon.[32]

Henry James did not fare as well, and his relationship to the Harpers was more complicated and problematic than Twain's or Howells.' Despite the fact that most of what James wrote before 1900 had been published in Harper periodicals before coming out in book form, James ultimately committed to Scribner's. Although James had sent a long synopsis of *The Ambassadors* to Harpers in 1900, it was shelved by Harvey and left untouched until Howells insisted on its quality. In 1903 Harpers began serializing the book in *The North American Review* and by November of that year Harpers published the entire book. The Harpers did not seem to treat James's texts with much courtesy and care; the house in fact lost one of the chapters of *The Ambassadors* and did not correct the error until 1950. While this was not the last James text published by the Harpers, James turned to Scribners for the "New York" edition of his complete works. Like Twain, James was able to see his works collected, organized, and published in a comprehensive set. Despite the fact that Harpers at least claimed to see more "merit" in Howells's texts than in James's, they were unable to offer him the same monument that Scribner's promised James.

For Howells and for his remaining readers, such a collection would have provided a valuable bridge across the gulf separating his "literature" and their lives. The author often used short pieces and articles to contextualize his larger works, and to position others within his vision of America's literary future. His introduction to the 1902 collection *Literature and Life,* part of the incomplete library edition, reaffirmed his convictions: "If I did not find life in what professed to be literature, I disabled its profession, and possibly from this habit, now inveterate with me, I am never quite sure of life unless I find literature in it." Literature, to Howells, was a force for the adhesion of communities, for the sharing of common experiences, pleasures, and sorrows. At its worst it was too idealistic, distracting from day-to-day social interactions, intoxicating, isolating, or misleading. His desire to see his works collected emerged from this same organizing impulse:

> . . . So it goes as to the motives and origins of the collection which may persist in disintegrating under the reader's eye, in spite of my well-meant endeavors to establish a solidarity for it. The group at least attests, even in this event, the wide, the wild, variety of my literary production in time and space . . . [33]

The parallel placement of "wide" and "wild" in this passage underscores the mixture of pride and anxiety Howells felt in regard to his life's work. Such a vast disorganized collection could permit—and even promote—misreading, misquotation, and misunderstanding.[34]

A primarily unannotated Howells has been read throughout this century. The tenets of literary realism recorded in his 1891 *Criticism and Fiction* are relatively well-known and widely read, but too often only partially anthologized, again the result of Howells's disorganized publication history. Historically read without guide, gloss, or context, the text has become more the product of a "Howells" than W. D. Howells; it has been stretched, clipped, and elliptically presented by Howells's critics and apologists since its publication, and readers have had few corrective resources. It seems reasonable to suggest that an authoritative collection of his works, edited and glossed by Howells himself, would have stabilized the significations of the piece.

Howells's reading of Dostoevsky in *Criticism and Fiction* clearly identifies the dominant vector of his poetics during and following the 1890s: "despite [Dostoevsky's] terrible picture of a soul's agony he is hopeful and wholesome, and teaches in every page patience, merciful judgment, humble helpfulness, and that brotherly responsibility, that duty of man to man, from which not even the Americans are emancipated." By choosing Dostoevsky, an author obsessed with the moral and social isolation of man faced the complexities and disillusionment of emerging modernity, Howells points to newer and subtler threats to American social reform. In an age of emergent imperialism, excessive capitalism, and spiritual crises, Howells strove to reposition literature as a pedagogical and emancipatory force.

It can be argued that *Criticism and Fiction* works, somewhat ambivalently, to recapture the social force most often associated with *Uncle Tom's Cabin* while rejecting out-of-hand the sentimentality of little Eva. Although this seems to suggest an impossibly tangled set of goals, Howells cuts the Gordian knot with a relatively simple sentence: "We invite our novelists," he writes, "to concern themselves with the more smiling aspects of life, which are the more American, and to seek the universal in the individual rather than the social interests." Both Howells's critics and his apologists have often become hopelessly trapped in the lackluster imagery of the first half of this sentence. It is, in fact, the second half that contains a key to reading his later works. By suggesting that writers seek the universal in the *individual* rather than the social interests, Howells returns to Emersonian self-reliance and Jeffersonian liberal democracy. According to this model, a good writer could be a teacher and an emancipator; he or she could free a mind from the corrupt paradigms of late-19th century capitalism and emergent imperialism simply by remaining "true to the facts."

Howells's organizing and controlling impulses worked not only to prevent errant receptions of his texts but also to contain ideological messiness and ambiguity. In the late 1880s and 1890s, at the peak of his own hegemony, Howells managed to maintain what he perceived to be a solid barrier between his business and his aesthetic interests. This reading departs from the generally accepted belief, most recently expressed by Michael Bell in *The Problem of American Realism* (1993), that *Criticism and Fiction* "apparently mattered far less to its author as an aesthetic manifesto than as an attempt to work out his own status as a writer, to reconcile the culturally divergent identities of 'artist' and 'man' by presenting authorship as one of what Jefferson called 'the real businesses of life.'"[35] It was, in fact, precisely "the businesses of life" that constantly impeded Howells's development as a writer. He saw himself as *capable* of a focused and directed artistic growth throughout the 1880s and 1890s, but only through a faithful dedication of time to imaginative fiction. His own submission to the pressures of the marketplace drove him to a statement of surrender to Aldrich in 1900:

> If I could have held out fifteen years ago in my refusal of the Study, when Alden tempted me, I might have gone on and beat *Silas Lapham*. Now I can only dream of some leisure day doing better . . . [36]

By 1900, Howells knew that he had fixed himself, through compounded (non-fiction) publishing contracts and obligations, in a kind of creative stasis. He would continue, until his death, to produce masses of material, but the volume of his productions hopelessly threatened his hopes for a creative evolution. Was Howells, as Bell suggests, using *Criticism and Fiction* and similar texts to align the signification of "authorship" with "business"? Yes, but this move was far less personal than Bell imagines. Howells used such texts—specifically *Criticism and Fiction* and *Literature and Life*—to create a new aesthetic vocabulary for his American readers; they were indeed "aesthetic manifestoes," born of personal urgencies but published for carefully planned public effects. "Authorship" was Howells's career; "literature" and "art" were Howells's elusive dreams. It is important that we separate these terms. Having done so, we can understand why, after working so hard to identify his career with respectable industry, Howells could write, only a few years after *Criticism and Fiction,* that "business is the opprobrium of literature."[37]

It would be illogical to argue that Howells felt somehow forced into a career of "authorship" and away from a literary life. Indeed, he was remarkably successful, financially and socially, in his adopted New England. Of his colleagues, only Twain made more money through shrewd self-promotion and strategic serialization. Howells liked making money, and he knew how to do it. His journals and letters from the period suggest, in fact, that Howells's greatest disappointments in his later years came not from any kind of artistic frustration or crisis but rather from his inability to find willing publishers for his fiction. He would be paid regularly, until his death, for his authorship of articles, reviews, columns, and essays, but by the late 1890s, his career as a producer of literature, as he understood it, was stalled at best. He had settled, even entrenched, himself into a fixed poetic that seemed increasingly tired to the industry that he had once dominated. He wrote sullenly to Twain in 1910: "one is so limp and helpless in the presence of the injustice which underlies society, and I am getting so old . . ."[38] Only travel writing and his "Easy Chair" columns provided Howells with a reasonably steadfast readership; other genres increasingly failed him. Even *Harper's*—to which Howells was required to submit all of his manuscripts first—rejected him outright in 1916. He wrote to Henry James: "A change has passed upon things, we can't deny it; I could not 'serialize' a story of mine now in any American magazine, thousands of them as there are."[39] These difficulties notwithstanding, falling silent was never an option that Howells entertained. Rather, he took stock of his diluted readership, studied the media and genres available to him, and worked to embed his social and aesthetic arguments within those structures to which he had access.

"I am as usual" Howells wrote in 1907, "busy making my gold-brick, without straw, buried in prosperous slavery to a salary and dreaming of some great achievement hereafter, well knowing that if any achievement of mine has greatness it [is] of heretofore."[40] These are the words of a man who imagines himself a victim of circumstance, without ambition, seemingly content to accept his "prosperous slavery." Cady argues that Howells had not "quit" at all, but was rather undervaluing himself publicly because he "fought egotism as the deadliest sin."[41]

In the first decade of the twentieth century, Howells began to allow a bit of "messiness" into his books. Socially dominant but ideologically residual, Howells could no longer maintain the wall between his literary and business careers: both were failing, and the energies he had for so long worked to separate now mingled to produce uniquely rich texts. His 1910 *Imaginary Interviews* contains a collection of such pieces from his Easy Chair columns. It is, characteristically, the "chair" itself that speaks in many of these pieces, and not the columnist. Howells increases the narrative distance even more by twisting genres and framing his arguments in dramatically constructed "interviews" and "conversations." The reader is, in short, invited to be amused and confused; only the most thoughtful would take the time to trace the agency of each argument through the many layers of genre, character, and narration.

In one of the text's more transparent moments, a venerable old author named Eugenio gives advice to aspiring writers:

> While we are still young we are aware of an environing and pervading censure, coming from the rivalry, the envy, the generous emulation, the approval, the disapproval, the love, the hate of all those who witness our endeavor. No smallest slip, no slightest defect will be lost upon this censure, equally useful whether sympathetic or antipathetic. But as we grow old we are sensible of a relaxing, a lifting, a withdrawal of the environing and pervading censure. We have become the objects of a compassionate toleration or a contemptuous indifference; it no longer matters greatly to the world whether we do our work well or ill . . . [42]

Eugenio's advice quickly becomes a kind of lament here. The narrative voice, suddenly slipping into a more personal "we" from the third-person mode of earlier paragraphs, allows a degree of connection between the reader and the usually distant Howells. This Howells, masked by Eugenio, sounds less concerned about his own failing creative energies than he is by the far more brutal "compassion" and "indifference" that have replaced "environing and pervading censure." The passage seems at once deeply honest and highly problematic: it suggests an aging Howells craving the censure that motivated and energized him in his youth but unwilling to commit to the kinds of writing needed to "merit" the censure of a twentieth century readership.

Eugenio appears again in chapter five of *Imaginary Interviews,* "The Unsatisfactoriness of Unfriendly Criticism": "The criticisms of one's books are always hard to bear if they are unfavorable, but he thought that displeasure for displeasure the earlier refusal to allow him certain merits was less displeasing than the later consent to take these merits for granted."[43] "Unfriendly Criticism" and in fact "unfriendly reading" are figured in this passage as presumptive reading: Eugenio acknowledges the complete lack of care with which readers now approach his texts. They are, again, regarded with compassion and polite interest but are not mined for new meanings or cultural relevance. His readers, Eugenio suggests, approach him *always* as a relic, and they approach his texts as the residue of a fading era.

Eugenio's meditations on criticism recall Dreiser's observation on Howells's generation; by situating the "problem" of his texts with their reception, Eugenio argues that the text is allowed to do cultural work only when unimpeded by the censure of trend: "With his own generation, with the readers who began young with him and have grown old with him, [the veteran author] is always safe. But there is a danger for him with the readers who begin young with him after he has grown old. It is they who find his tales twice told and himself hackneyed, unless they have been trained to like his personal quality by their elders. This might be difficult, but not impossible, and ought not it to be the glad, the grateful care of such elders?"[44] This attempt to locate a "personal quality" that transcends generational difference seems strained at best. Through Eugenio, Howells betrays his divided consciousness on the issue of his own relevance. He suggests on the one hand that young readers look past his archaic "personal quality" and mine his works for current material, and on the other hand he asks that young readers learn to appreciate his craft, defunct as it may seem to their jaded eyes.

"The Critical Bookstore" is one of a body of self-reflective works of fiction that Howells produced in the twentieth century. It is certainly the one that documents most directly his imaginative helplessness before the new literary marketplace. A number of Howells's readers have attributed his increasing self-reflection to the many deaths that surrounded him during these years: he lost his father, his daughter, his wife, his close friend Samuel Clemens. Especially after 1910, Howells entered an autobiographical phase that crossed genres. *New Leaf Mills* (1913), a text he started as "New Arcady Mills" in 1867, is the clearest example of Howells twentieth-century attempts to reconcile his personal past with his professional persona. In his collection of essays on Howells entitled *The Mask of Fiction,* John Crowley uses the publication of *New Leaf Mills* as a marker for an important shift in Howells's poetics:

> Here, near the end of his career, Howells was distinguishing in theory between two kinds of writing he had already tried to distinguish in practice: *autobiography,* in which the figure of the self tends to dissolve into the carpet of family and world; *fiction,* in which the self is figured by

concealment and thereby retains its lineaments. Paradoxically, the self-portraiture of autobiography effaces the self, while the mask of fiction reveals its face.[45]

As Crowley suggests, the most revealing kind of narrative for a reader of Howells is situated on the boundary between fiction and autobiography. Many of Howells's texts fit this description, including of course *The Rise of Silas Lapham* and *A Hazard of New Fortunes,* but it is the post-1910 body of work, particularly "The Critical Bookstore," *Imaginary Interviews,* and *New Leaf Mills,* that self consciously engages with this boundary as a subject. Facing his own uncertain status and imperiled legacy, Howells worked to place himself within a series of imagined communities, not the least of which was his own family.

It is not surprising that Howells began but never finished an "official" autobiography during these same years. *Years of My Youth* (1916), the first volume of the incomplete three-part series, presents itself as a nostalgic fireside chat but masks an often sharply polemical dimension. The tone is often perceptibly angry; the inflection of the title changes after a careful reading: "my" becomes stressed rather than "youth." Howells sets his autobiography against the lives he sees developing around him, the "youth" of America around 1916. The text's ostensible subject and purpose—essentially the meditations of an old man on distant places and forgotten years—gives Howells the opportunity to build his arguments into strong and safe narrative structures. A significant portion of the text documents the years just preceding and during the Civil War. Unlike Henry Adams, whose autobiographical *Education* emerged and was widely read during the same years, Howells does not explicitly compare the chaotic uncertainties of the present with a more directed and unified past. Instead, he reads the two into each other, finding them more similar than he or his readers may wish to admit:

> . . . though the war against slavery tried to believe itself a war for the Union, when it came to full consciousness it knew itself a war for freedom; such freedom, lame and halt, as we have been able to keep for the negroes; a war for democracy, such democracy as we shall not have for ourselves until we have an economic democracy . . . [46]

The passage speaks to Howells's ambivalent reaction to the first World War. Cast as a war against tyranny, in support of democracy, Howells had difficulty seeing the war as anything but the inevitable outcome of years of international imperialism. "A war for democracy" whether domestic or global, would serve questionable ends unless it helped to recreate and redefine the very democracy it strove to protect and to spread.[47] It is impossible to ignore the fact that the war—even before the United States' entrance into it—radically affected Howells's literary and political imaginations. His frustrations with the literary marketplace paralleled closely his frustrations with the failure of American democracy: he saw both as corrupted by immense economic pressures and interests.

Howells knew, and clearly seemed to accept, that social change could only take place with the support, motivation, and enthusiasm of the nation's youth. Youth governed trend and dominated the literary tastes of the public more than it had in his early years. The literary canon was no longer driven and determined by the tastes of a narrow Boston or New York elite. The once revered genealogy of *Atlantic Monthly* and *Harper's* editors had long since lost its automatic cache with young authors who had a variety of alternative resources and, more significantly, agents to consult. The author had become as much of a commodity as his or her book, and to Howells this represented a significant threat to the pedagogical dimension of reading and writing. The young author, he worried, would forget his or her responsibility to the craft of writing and to the community of individuals for which he or she wrote.

Howells sets the print culture of 1916 into dialogue with the print culture of the 1840s in *Years of My Youth*. Thanks to his father, William Cooper Howells, Howells had some knowledge of the art and business of printing. Although most evidence from his letters, journals, and fiction (*New Leaf Mills*) points to the fact that Howells did not remember fondly his father's attempts at paper-making and amateur printing in the 1840s, he addresses the subject positively in *Years of My Youth*. Howells uses the text, in fact, to romanticize print as an art and craft worthy of Stickly or Wright:

> From a quaint pride [my father] did not like his printer's craft to be called a trade; he contented that it was a profession; he was interested in it, as the expression of his taste, and the exercise of hi ingenuity and invention, and he could supply many deficiencies in its means and processes . . . Nothing pleased him more than to contrive a thing out of something it was not meant for. . . . He could do almost anything with his ready hand and his ingenious brain, while I have never done anything with mine but write a few score books . . . [48]

A few score books? The direct comparison Howells makes between his own craft and his father's seems hardly necessary here: the passage relies on the connection between past and present, on the conflation of things "old" with things "ingenious" and "ready." *Years of My Youth* is both an autobiography and an antimodern declaration; it is a text that works against modernity by elevating writing first to the level of "craft" and then to the level of "profession," openly defying the modern proliferation of mass-produced journals, magazines, and newspapers. A liability earlier in his career, Howells's lack of formal education now became an asset: "the printing-office was mainly my school."[49]

Among his earliest influences, in *Years of My Youth* Howells counts Poe and Defoe highest, writing that in his tenth or eleventh year he was "enlarging [his] sense of human events through *Gulliver's Travels* and Poe's *Tales of the Grotesque and Arabesque*."[50] Howells assures the twentieth-century reader of *Years of My Youth* that he grew up without the Puritanical strictures that seemed to limit his adult canon: "[my father] may have thought that no harm could come to me from the literary filth which I sometimes took into my mind, since it was in the nature of sewage to purify itself."[51] Though this confession comes before Van Wyck Brooks's 1918 accusation that Howells was something of a prude, it does reflect the anxiety that his art was, if not only behind-the-times, utterly defunct and unable to penetrate a readership conditioned for sensationalism.[52] He tried, in his autobiography, to demonstrate a certain capacity, if not a tolerance, for filth.

Curiously, the crime that Howells cites in his young self is *vanity,* and it is this same crime that he projects forward to the young writers of the early twentieth century: "Vanity so criminal as ours, might have been for a just punishment lastingly immured in that village which the primeval woods encircled like a prison wall. . . ."[53] Later in *Years of My Youth* he speaks more generally of the narrow vision of immature authors: "The best that could be said of [the young writers] was that so far as they knew the right, they served it . . . they got their fun out of the opportunities which the situation offered, and they did not believe the worst was coming."[54] The only remedy for such vanity was an understanding that truly excellent literature receives "slow acclaim," not the "prompt acclaim the drama enjoys."[55] It is striking that Howells addresses his younger self together with the newer generation here. Following a pattern begun by Eugenio in *Imaginary Interviews,* Howells indicts himself along with the modern writer, speaking with both the authority of age and experience and with the familiarity made possible by situating himself within an imagined community of timeless writers.

Especially in 1916, the year of Henry James's death, Howells must have acutely felt the distance between his waning powers and the vigorous and altogether alien literary culture that allowed the success in America of such writers as Fitzgerald, Lewis, and Dreiser. Howells had called for a gradual evolution of literary taste and production and he had witnessed nothing less than a revolution; his own important role in these rapid transformations was by his eightieth year largely unrecognized. He knew himself to be, at least beside Henry James, "comparatively a dead cult with . . . statues cut down and the grass growing over them in the pale moonlight."[56]

Chapter Four

The Leatherwood God and *My Mark Twain*: The Importance of Samuel Clemens in Howells's Literary Imagination after 1910

> I find largely that Tolstoy was right when in trying to furnish reminiscences for his biographer he declared that remembering was Hell: with the little brave and good you recall so much bad and base . . .
> —W. D. Howells to John Mead Howells, 12 January 1914.[1]

Upon the death of his friend and confidant Samuel Clemens in April, 1910, William Dean Howells embarked on what would be his most rapid and least revised literary endeavor. Within forty days of Clemens's death, Howells produced the entire manuscript of *My Mark Twain*, a text that even some of his harshest critics would extol as sensitive and powerful. *The Nation*, a journal habitually critical of Howells, ran a review of the text praising it as "a vivid picture . . . of a rare friendship between two richly endowed natures."[1] Howells expressed a characteristic mixture of satisfaction and anxiety upon the text's publication in *Harper's Monthly:* "I am sensitive of much raw haste in [*My Mark Twain*], and perhaps a braggy note;" despite the extent and frequency of his production in the twentieth century, Howells rarely moved from composition to publication in fewer than six months. He tended rather to overlap numerous projects, not the least pressing of which was his monthly commitment to the "Editor's Easy Chair." *My Mark Twain* provides a unique example of a Howells composition virtually unaltered by his probing self-doubt and tendency to obsessive revision. Behind his "raw" representation of Clemens, Howells leaves an autobiographical shadow, a trace of the complex of anxieties and hopes which drove his fiction in his final decade of life.

This chapter will analyze the significance and force of Clemens in Howells's literary imagination after 1910. Not limited to elegiac prose or to biography, Howells's remembrances of Clemens enriched his later prose, reinvigorating projects he had long since abandoned as fragments of youthful idealism. Vexed both by Clemens's indefatigable nonconformity and popular appeal, Howells would turn his fictional attention to these subjects as he continued his decades-long analysis of the aesthetic tastes and capriciousness of the American reader. His 1916 novel *The Leatherwood God,* written in the years following *My Mark Twain,* explores the near-hypnotic influence of Joseph Dylks—a messianic pretender—over a backwoods Ohio town in the early nineteenth century. At once a work of historical fiction and a study of the gullibility and spiritual hunger of the American people, *The Leatherwood God* offers a lengthy and cautious study of personality and persuasion. Howells's representation of Dylks, "towering over those near him . . . his hair tossed like a mane on his shoulders" (20), recalls Clemens's commanding presence as it taps an ideal of frontier hardiness. Joseph Dylks, part madman, part preacher, a figure of Lincolnian stature commanding a comparable cult of personality, emerges somewhat unexpectedly from Howells's imagination. He is a figure without precedent in more than fifty years of production: appearing mysteriously from the backwoods and transforming all those he encounters, more raw and masculine than Bartley Hubbard, void of the inevitable autobiographical attachments carried by March and Lapham, and perhaps most significantly, utterly impervious to the vocabularies of class and material culture.

Dylks is not Clemens; he is rather an exaggerated expression of that aspect of Clemens's private and public persona that Howells labeled "histrionic:" the sense of theatre that both created and sustained his appeal. *The Leatherwood God* is a study of Clemens only insofar as it is a reflection by Howells on those characteristics that he lacked utterly, the sense of showmanship and the animated devotion to ideas that worked to create a cult of personality. Howells would continue to reprove such tendencies formally, and he regarded *The Leatherwood God*—at least publicly—as a record of a "dreadful imposture,"[2] but the text is most interesting when regarded as an effort to explore and contain his increasing recognition of the power of the histrionic on the American mind.

Not surprisingly, *My Mark Twain* provides numerous examples of this gradual acceptance. In one of his most revealing and uncharacteristic passages, Howells writes that Twain "was realistic, but he was essentially histrionic, and he was rightly so. What we have strongly conceived we ought to make others strongly imagine, and we ought to use every genuine art to that end" (52).[3]

The imprecision of this comment betrays something of its author's uncertainties at the time of composition, but the syntax does, when untangled, reveal a logical connection between "histrionic" and "genuine art," a formula both unexpected and highly suggestive in a text by Howells. The use of the first person plural, anomalous in this or any biography, identifies a particularly strong self-reflective dimension in the text, both a harbinger of the decade of autobiography to follow and a reinforcement of the possessive in the book's title.

Howells's attention to his own legacy emerges forcefully in *My Mark Twain*. With most of his contemporaries dead or dying in 1910, his authorial voice developed an elegiac character not dissimilar to the one adopted by his own critics and reviewers. Acutely aware that his "statues" had been "cut down," and embittered by the absence of the veneration he himself had seen thirty years before for Holmes, Longfellow, and Emerson (despite the latter's dementia), Howells approached his texts with one eye to the future and the other to a notion that he could bring his oeuvre to some sort of idealized closure. The failure of the library edition and his publishers' resistance to serialization of his later works served to reinforce his sense of irrelevance and render more urgent his drive to conclude and package his life's productions and fragmented public persona. Van Wyck Brooks, who produced to most comprehensive record of anti-Howells rhetoric, remarks that he came to be treated, by 1910, "as a valley of humiliation between two mountains of pride—the mountains being Henry James and Mark Twain."[4]

Brooks's level of hyperbole notwithstanding, Howells's engagement with the problem of fame found expression in his fictional study of proselytizers and in his representations of the pathos of individuals victimized by the intensity of their beliefs.[5] Neither *My Mark Twain* nor *The Leatherwood God* celebrate histrionics, but both release and ultimately contain powerful personalities who destabilize and transform lives and institutions, defying order and expectation, and ultimately collapse under the unsustainable weight of the facades they worked to maintain. It is significant that contemporary reviewers in the *New York Times* and *The Nation* made a series of connections between *The Leatherwood God* and Clemens's *The Mysterious Stranger,* but it even more remarkable that so few studied Howells's emulation of his friend's technique in the text. Clara and Rudolf Kirk provide the only critical reference to the transformation in Howells's style and approach: "Except for the fact that the figure of Dylks is appalling in its gaunt fanaticism and cowardice, and the figure of the King in *Huckleberry Finn* is hilariously funny to the point of ribaldry, one might think that the adventure at Leatherwood Creek was merely another chapter in Twain's tale of a backwoods community somewhere along the Mississippi."[6]

Howells himself would make no mention of Clemens's style or personality in connection with his composition of *Leatherwood*; his silence on the subject seems particularly suggestive in light of the incontrovertible parallels between Dylks's activities in Leatherwood and the King's and Duke's enactment of a mock religious revival in *Huckleberry Finn*. While he avoided mention of Clemens's literary fascination with the huckster, Howells devoted significant time and space in his reviews and biographical sketches of Clemens to discussing the latter's own tendency to locate, extol, and ultimately promote products devoted to curing the "ills" of individuals or American society in general. Clemens, Howells writes in *My Mark Twain*, would pursue the salvation and redemption of "the damned human race" (and the lining of his own pockets) through any number of questionable gimmicks ranging from a "panacea" called plasmon, to his experiments with print technology and the promotion of a biography of Pope Leo XIII to legions of Catholics who "could not read" and "might not wish to read" (73). The tone of Howells's descriptions of Clemens's enterprises betrays a fond dissatisfaction; he observes simply that this was "an interesting phase of [Clemens's] psychology," one that became more prominent with age. Such passionate spontaneity—so distant from Howells's own experience—emerge in *My Mark Twain* as a source of tremendous aesthetic potency and personal risk:

> When filled up with an experience that deeply interested him, or when provoked by some injustice or absurdity that intensely moved him, [Clemens] burst forth, and the outbreak might be altogether humorous, but it was more likely to be humorous with a groundswell of seriousness carrying it profoundly forward.[7]

Howells traces in Clemens a tendency to take some personal desire—pecuniary, political, spiritual—and translate it into a crusade. Far removed from Howells's own fractious efforts to merge social and self-interest, Clemens manages the paradox through a theatrics of public personality; he is able to "burst forth" with full expressive energy in response to whim and is therefore free from the constant pressure Howells imposed on himself to reconcile the private life of the artist with the broader arc of his productions.

It is this ability to manage and embrace contradiction, crucial to the richness and success of Clemens's humor and writing, that dominates Howells's posthumous representation of him. He cites Clemens's sense of complicity with those institutions he criticized and even worked to undermine, including the "Roman Church" and the fledgling Christian Scientist movement:

. . . Clemens was building his engines of war for the destruction of Christian Science, which superstition nobody, and he least of all, expected to destroy. It would not be easy to say whether in his talk of it his disgust for the illiterate twaddle of Mrs. Eddy's book, or his admiration for her genius for organization was the greater. He believed that as a religious machine the Christian Science Church was as perfect as the Roman Church and destined to be more formidable in its control of the minds of men. He looked for its spread all over the whole of Christendom, and throughout the winter he spent at Riverdale he was ready to meet all listeners more than half-way with his convictions of its powerful grasp of the average human desire to get something for nothing. The vacuous vulgarity of its texts were a perpetual joy to him, while he bowed with serious respect to the sagacity which built so securely upon the everlasting rock of human credulity and folly . . . (84)

This marked contrast between Howells's faith in human rationality—flagging as it was in 1910—and Clemens's rich cynicism creates the meaningful center of *My Mark Twain*. The elegy offers Howells an occasion for aesthetic transition, a movement toward and vocabulary for cynicism and a critique of the American public entirely unavailable to him twenty years before. His reawaked interest in the "Leatherwood Creek" project followed closely on the publication of *My Mark Twain,* and its four years of serious development and composition represent a process of reflection on the meaning of Samuel Clemens in his literary imagination.

Throughout this process Howells hoped to protect the integrity of his realist legacy by adopting an integrated view of the historical and realistic novel. He presumed that an historical novel—even an historical *romance*—could be written independent of any commitment to a new literary aesthetic, and that it could then be rationalized in the realistic terms of *Criticism and Fiction*. As it turned out, Howells's attempt to adopt a new voice in the novels involved him in unexpected critical inquiries into the nature of the realistic novel and produced reviews announcing (surely to his surprise) an incipient romantic tendency in his works. The Leatherwood project emerges synchronously with his conversations with Clemens on the subject of autobiography and its force in and behind fictional production. In response to Howells's famous 1904 letter to Clemens about the dangers of expressing "the black heart's truth" in literature, the latter remarked: "The remorseless truth *is* there, between the lines, where the author-cat is raking dust upon it which hides from the disinterested spectator neither it nor its smell . . . the reader knows the writer in spite of his wily diligences."[8] Less than a month later

Howells sent inquiries to his brother John and sister Aurelia seeking information on the history of the Leatherwood affair.[9]

The intertextual nature of *The Leatherwood God* provided Howells with both a forum for stylistic experimentation and an alibi for aesthetic deviance. Although he would claim different levels of indebtedness at different times, the novel was undeniably based largely on Richard H. Tanneyhill's "The Leatherwood God. An Account of the Appearances and Pretensions of Joseph C. Dylks in Eastern Ohio in 1828." Published in the *Ohio Valley Historical Series* and reviewed by Howells in the August 1871 *Atlantic Monthly*, Tannyhill's narrative provided Howells with the frame, some characters, the title, and the subject of his novel. In 1897 Howells included mention of the episode in *Stories of Ohio*, a school reader, writing that the history of early Ohio was surrounded by "a teasing sense of . . . obscurity" and that the history of the early settlers represented "the beginning of a mighty history" inseparable from "the life of the whole race."[10] The "Publisher's Note" to the 1916 edition of *The Leatherwood God* acknowledges the narrative's complex history and evolution:

> The Author thinks it well to appraise the reader that the historical outline of this story is largely taken from the admirable narrative of Judge Tanneyhill in the *Ohio Valley Series,* Robert Clarke Co., Cincinnati. The details are often invented, and the characters are all invented as to their psychological evolution, though some are based upon those of real persons easily identifiable in that narrative. The drama is that of the actual events in its main development; but the vital incidents, or the vital uses of them, are the author's. At times he has enlarged them; at times he has paraphrased the accounts of the witnesses; in one instance he has frankly reproduced the words of the imposter as reported by one who heard Dylks's last address in the Temple at Leatherwood and as given in the Tanneyhill narrative. Otherwise the story is effectively fiction. (2)[11]

Howells's use of the Ohio narrative to produce an historical novel mirrors his autobiographical projects in those same years in that he would draw from the structured memories provided by journals, letters, and family recollections and infuse them with a "vital fiction." *The Leatherwood God,* a narrative unfettered by any ostensible autobiographical connections, was fertile ground for experimentation and reflection enriched by its western setting. The Ohio of the novel was known to Howells but not uncomfortably linked to his own past, it represented a rawness of experience and an aesthetic freedom from his New England and New York associations. As such, memories of the Leatherwood episode occupied the same imaginative space as memories of

Clemens. He wrote to his sister Aurelia at the beginning of a summer devoted entirely to the work: "After a long season of autobiography I have resumed my story of *The Leatherwood God,* that strange episode of Ohio history which has always fascinated me; but the dreadfulness and the mystery of the imposture rather distresses me, and I wish I had some cheerfuller theme . . . I find that there is a distinct flagging in my mental force, either from age, or from the constant work of fifty or sixty years."[12]

Part of this weariness surely extended from Howells's certitude that his novel would be met with a lukewarm critical response at best and his sense that it would be difficult to serialize. He wrote to Duneka on September 23, 1914 to notify of the text's completion: "I have finished a novel (historical, oddly enough) which I have thought of for forty years and got well started thirty years ago . . . I think it rather well done, but there is no 'love interest' of the merchantable sort, though there is the pathos of a grim woman's wrong, (*not* seduction.). The structure is almost wholly fact . . ."[13] Howells's letters to Duneka are often marked by evasions and more particularly by his highly self-conscious considerations of contract. Here his letter reveals a strong sense of his female audience and his publishers concerns over satisfying that demographic. The letter's most interesting feature is its reference to getting the novel "well started thirty years ago." It is highly improbable that Howells devoted any energy whatsoever to the composition or even the development of *The Leatherwood God* before 1900, except of course his work reviewing and excerpting the Tanneyhill text for various publications. Because of his binding contract with Harpers, Howells was required to give them first access to his works; he knew well, however, that the house had little interest in serializing his novels and would more likely limit their involvement to the publication of a book-length version.[14] It was crucial for Howells to claim—as often as possible—that the novel had been conceived before his binding contract with Harper & Brothers. This permitted him a measure of flexibility and a chance at financial gain as well as the increased visibility granted by serial publication. In the end he triumphed and wrote his daughter on November 2, 1915: "Duneka conceded all rights to *The Leatherwood God* in view of the fact that it was imagined and actually begun before my Harvey contract." The text was serialized in *The Century* the following year.

This mixture of imaginative weariness and aggressive self-promotion demonstrates again Howells's growing sense of the divided office of authorship. "Apparently," he writes in 1911, "there are two selves of the one novelist who are simultaneously writing fiction entirely opposed in theory and practice."[15] The tension produced by this dualistic self-conception contributes to the "distress" he cites in letters to his family in the years just following

Clemens's death, and his expressions of this tension reveal a preoccupation with the degradation of his once sturdy optimism, understood here as a "flagging" of mental energies linked to dark tones and "dreadful" themes. While turning with a characteristic candor to his sister Aurelia's sympathies, Howells fronts a very different persona when he writes to Henry James of his novel claiming "to have more muscle than for some years past, for that sort of work."[16] Uneasily imagining his reputation as a vigorous, productive author while enduring the failings of age and the inevitable criticism of a younger set to antiquated ideas and authority, his use of terms of physical strength and weakness also suggests Howells's anxiety concerning his ability to manage a negotiation of the personal and the imaginative in his fiction. Viewed within this context, the Leatherwood project simultaneously reinforces and threatens Howells's authorial identity through its palimpsestic nature. His only example of a novelistic synthesis of autobiography, historical recreation, and realist expression, *The Leatherwood God* is an evocation of Clemens's unclassifiable fiction that imaginatively reestablish Howells as a "frontier" writer capable of an aesthetic totally free of bourgeois significations and representations. In a letter to Henry James Jr., son of William, Howells, again ignoring the lack of originality in *The Leatherwood God,* tries to bring to the book the same timely cultural significance he had expected—and in some measure experienced—with *A Hazard of New Fortunes.* Pointing out his reading of William James's posthumously published *Some Problems of Philosophy* (1911) during the composition of his novel, Howells writes, "if I do not find the meaning and the moral of The Leatherwood God amidst its wonderful commonsense psychology, it will be my fault."[17]

He had expressed the same desire to share intellectual space with William James during the composition of *A Hazard of New Fortunes,* and while it is unclear whether Howells wished to find a reiteration of some already established theme in *Some Problems of Philosophy* or to enrich his work with Jamesian ideas, the texts do inform one another. William James's effort to confront and refute objections to the study of philosophy speak clearly to Howells's reevaluation of his more restrained aesthetic:

> *Objection 3:* Philosophy is out of touch with real life, for which it substitutes abstractions. The real world is various, tangled, painful. Philosophers have, almost without exception, treated it as noble, simple, perfect, ignoring the complexity of fact, and indulging in a sort of optimism that exposes their systems to the contempt of common men . . .

> *Reply.* This objection also is historically valid, but no reason appears why philosophy should keep aloof from reality permanently. Her manners

may change as she successfully develops . . . In the end philosophers may
get into as close contact as realistic novelists with the facts of life . . .

Imagining himself somewhere between the "philosopher" and the "realistic novelist" figured in this passage, Howells would have felt some complicity with James's admission of the philosopher's "substitution of abstractions"
for life's "various, tangled, and painful" elements. Largely the result of the
massive influx of Freudian psychology into the American literary landscape,
the increasing demand on writers to probe deeply into the "black heart's
truth" left him with a stark choice: Capable of writing experimental novels,
Howells was forced to decide the extend to which he would distance himself
from his own past works. Would he attempt—at a very advanced age—to become a "new" Howells, to reimagine his aesthetic and market himself differ-
ently, or would he rely on the hope that his legacy would transcend trend and
stabilize in some unforeseeable future? His first biographer, Alexander
Harvey, writing in 1915 and 1916, offered very little hope for a reliable representation in America's cultural and literary memory:

> To tell the truth, it is impossible to read the literature of the psychoana-
> lytic school of Freudian psychology without marveling at the complete-
> ness with which the whole fabric of the Howells criticism collapses and
> disintegrates. It is all surface and no depth . . . [Howells] has done an
> enormous amount of damage to American literature . . . The poverty of
> the American Anglo-Saxon mind consists in this very superficiality, this
> strict adherence to the surface of life . . . [18]

The Leatherwood God responds to this call for "depth" most simply by adopting a prefabricated surface; Howells would spare his imaginative energies for
the development of character and for probing into psychology and motivation. Enriched by its proximity to the composition of autobiography, this
composition process clearly yielded unexpected results. Howells would mention with uncharacteristic frequency his debt to Tanneyhill, referring to the
supporting narrative far more often than the etiquette and conventions of intellectual property mandated. "I am almost ashamed to think how little *The
Leatherwood God* owes to my invention," he wrote to a reader in Maine, "almost" ashamed because the experiment briefly reignited his celebrity and
prompted some degree of reevaluation of his development and legacy.[19] He
had proved that, like James's philosophy, his "manners could change" and
"successfully develop."

As John Crowley Jr. suggests in *The Dean of American Letters,* all of
Howells's productions in the final decade of his life worked to some extent to

counter the increasingly popular use of his name and image as an emblem for the "supposed feminization of American culture." He could do little to counter the *ad hominem* attacks (sometimes packaged as "appreciations") of Dreiser, Norris, Anderson, the less known Freudians, and especially H.L. Mencken and Van Wyck Brooks. A simultaneous projection and critique of great physical strength and vigor, Howells's Joseph Dylks stands as a peculiar complex of Clemens's theatrical magnetism and a near caricature of the hyper-masculine, defined by his *very* brief—if intense—impact on the Leatherwood community.

Both Pattison and Crowley Jr. provide comprehensive accounts of the critical response to *The Leatherwood God.* Mencken identified the work's "shallow" feel, its avoidance of the "profound dread and agony of life, the surge of passion and aspiration, the grand crash and glitter of things, the tragedy that runs eternally under the surface."[20] Howells's evaluation of his text's reception betrays his mounting frustration with domestic audiences, a dissatisfaction dating back to *Hazard.* "Have you read the Leatherwood God?" he asks Anne Frechette late in 1916, "The English have received it intelligently, and the American critics though kind, most ignorantly. What strange animals some of them are."

Among the most effective passages in *The Leatherwood God* are those in which the narrator analyzes the credulity of Dylks's "converts:"

> Day by day the faith in Dylks spread with circumstance which strengthened it in the converts; they accepted the differences which parted husband, wife, parent and child, and set strife between brothers and neighbors as proof of his divine authority to bring a sword; they knew by the hate and dissension which followed his claim that it was of supernatural force, and when the pillars of the old spiritual temples fell one after another under his blows, they exulted in the ruin as the foundation of a new sanctuary . . . (53)

Energized by dissent, his message made meaningful by the substance of the negative response it incites, Dylks stands at once as an illustration of the American jeremiad and as a figure through which the text engages with the twentieth-century American desire to locate meaning in the divisive and negative energies within self and community. Dylks's sensationalism is precisely his appeal; his counter-cultural exhortations, functionally meaningless, drive the mass to respond "We shall never die!" and "behold our God!" (55).

Vacillating between revivalist discourse and the critical perspective of Squire Braile, the text builds a structure of cynical self-reflection into the narrative enriched by Braile's sardonic voice: "This new deity isn't going to be satisfied with worship merely. Money, of course, he'll want and get, and he'll wear purple and fine linen, and feed upon fried chicken every day" (57). The text encircles the dialectic created between the unchecked spiritual aspirations of Dylks and Braile's atheism. Both men are trapped by a system of belief: Dylks by his elaborate public- and self-deception and Braile by his inescapable sense of irony founded in enlightenment thinking and texts. Historically alienated from Leatherwood's complex of Christian sects (primarily Methodists and "United Brethren,") Braile serves not only as Justice of the Peace but also as a town skeptic. He "alone had the courage to disable their judgment which he liked to say was no more infallible than so much scripture, but the hardy infidel who knew so much law, and was inexpugnable in his office, owed that he could not make head against their gospel. He could darken their counsel with citations from *Common Sense* and *The Age of Reason,* but the piety of the community remained safe from his mockery" (40). While most often viewed as a mouthpiece for Howells or even as a chorus of impartiality behind the text's primary narrative, Braile is most interesting when considered as a commentary on stasis, unproductiveness, and even solipsism. He hardly leaves his front porch in the book, limiting his involvement to bemused reaction and meditation on the foolishness of the townspeople. When, at the opening of the text, his neighbor Abel Reverdy enters into a lengthy and animated description of Dylks's activities, Braile "smokes tranquilly" with "indifference" and "amiable condescension" (11).

Subverting readers' expectations, the text allows Dylks some degree of development and dynamism while limiting Braile to the position of observer/commentator. The town and its systems of class, faith, and education find a peculiarly theatrical expression in the book with the Temple—an interdemoninational religious hall—as the single space in which competing voices achieve a strange consensus through dissent. By offering up the image of the Temple, or more generally the place of religious gathering, as the locus of an American theatre which plays out and resolves difference in community, Howells positions his text within the long tradition of conversations among literary, political, and religious cultures. The world of the temple is entirely theatrical:

> At the first meeting in the Temple after the open return of Dylks to his dispensation, the Little Flock had apparently suffered no loss in number. Some of his followers had left him, but his disciples had been busily preaching him during his abeyance, and the defection of old converts was more than made up by the number of proselytes. The room actually left by the Flock was filled by the Herd of the Lost who occupied all of

> the seats on the one side of the Temple, with Matthew Braile and his wife in a foremost place, the lower sort of them worsening into the Hounds who filled the doorway, and hung about the outside of the Temple . . . the whole assembly was orderly. Those of the Little Flock who conducted the services had a quelled air, which might have been imparted on them by the behavior of Dylks; he sat bowed and humble on the bench below the pulpit, while Enraghty preached above him. It was rumored that at the house-meetings the worship of Dylks had been renewed with the earlier ardor; there had been genuflections and prostrations before him . . . (126)

A description more characteristic of Pepys than Howells, the passage signifies the text's broad interest in the dynamics of the frontier community, a community drawn in thick strokes and divided among named sects: the boisterous and blasphemous "Hounds," the cowed "Little Flock." By mapping and vectoring the shifting shapes and interests of these groups, the text unfolds as a cynical record of credulity on the one hand and an analysis of cults of personality on the other.

The longest and among the only published readings of *The Leatherwood God,* the closing chapter of Elizabeth Prioleau's *The Circle of Eros* (1983) explicates the novel as a playing out of Howells's sexual and professional neuroses:

> Concealed within this triumphant sexual fable is another success story: Howells's own. Covertly, the novel provides a dramatization of an achievement as large as Leatherwood's erotic ethic, his own self-integration. The two, of course, go hand-in-hand; but compressed into the text is a telling account of his personal, creative growth. .he confronts the heart of his inner darkness through Dylks and his scourge . . . the classic encounter with the unconscious necessary for psychic wholeness. . . . [21]

Prioleau's argument that *The Leatherwood God* represents a "bringing into final coherence" Howells's lifelong "erotic investigations" is not incompatible with an understanding of the text as an expression of the artist's relationship with audience and more specifically of Howells's sense of his readership. Especially after 1900, Howells became increasingly aware of the parallels between his understanding of sexuality and his theories of reading. Driven in part by the Freudian "Psychological Counter-Current," he remarked a 1902 article for the *North American Review* entitled "Will the Novel Disappear?," "it is probable that the psychological novel will be the most enduring as it has been the most constant phase of fiction. Every other kind of novel lives or dies by so much or so little psychology as it has in it."[22] The "psychology it has in it," signifies a text's degree of attention to and engagement with issues of sex and death, of Eros and Thanatos. By figuring here the novel itself as something that "lives or dies," Howells suggests a similarly psychologized understanding of writing and reading. Squire Braile impassively "reads" Dylks; the various peoples of Leatherwood "read" his message of salvation into their own lives, and *The Leatherwood God* achieves a new level of theatrics. It dramatizes the sexualized author-reader relationship and explores the desire that brings a reader to a given text or subject and the author's fantasy fulfillment of that desire. Squire Braile's ironic detachment from this erotic dynamic is exposed in the novel as strained. As Prioleau suggests, Braile's cynicism "mellows and he gains a grasp of the dark intricacies and compulsions of the irrational" (176).

Living in his log cabin, so perfectly structured and centralized in the community, (like "Howells's books" as Proileau remarks) with its chained raccoon and carefully restrained emotions, Braile becomes increasingly agitated as Dylks gains followers in Leatherwood. The only breaks in his stolidity accompany his brief and halting references to his recently dead son, significant in their proximity to Freudian denial. The text stops short of heroicizing his repressive impassivity just as it stops short of rendering tragic Dylks's rapid descent toward self-recognition. *The Leatherwood God* lacks a tragic or a heroic structure; it adopts, rather, the dialectic between destructive self-deification (Dylks) and cynical self-denial (Braile) and places both in a critical light. When the Leatherwood community begins to collapse, it does so because of an imbalance in this structure that fractures the integrity of family, class, and political consciousness. Howells's novel presents the life of the town as a theatre that requires some willing suspension of self-interest and some blind faith in a system of laws—spiritual and civic—paradoxically born of free will *and* imposed by some far away power.

Examined in this manner, *The Leatherwood God*, like so many of Howells's novels, enacts a dramatization of the formation of individual in a democracy. The novel is most unusual in its engagement with those forces Howells would have called "psychological" and in its resistance to surface details. The conflict between Dylks and Braile, a struggle that appears moralistic until its uneasy resolution, emerges in clear relief against the bold depictions of the "Hounds" and other broadly painted social groups. There are very few clear voices in the text, and those who speak categorize themselves easily through the degree and nature of their dialect. Abel Reverdy, the most verbose character in the text, emerges as almost clownish through a combination of his backwoods colloquialisms and Braile's intolerance of him. He is among the few of his class given a voice at all in the text. The poor of

Leatherwood, divided for the most part among the various categories of rab-
ble, swing witlessly from camp to camp, listening to Braile's references to literature and law with the same blind reverence they offer to Dylks. Lacking
education, wealth, and perhaps most crucial in the frontier town, land, the
majority of the townspeople appear in the novel as noisy groundlings, com-
menting randomly on the action, determining to some extent the success of
the drama, but granted no individual expression. If the text forwards some
sort of judgment on this group it is an echo of Clemens's declamations on the
"damned human race." Never sinister, sometimes violent, always foolish, the
crowd follows its perceived spiritual and intellectual leaders without regard to
consequence and with a desperate desire for "salvation," however the term
may be defined at a given moment.

While the voiceless poor drive the novel to resolution by engaging in
sudden and powerful actions (the shredding of the "seamless raiment," the
near lynching of Dylks), they move in response to the decisions of those
townspeople who claim higher social or economic station. Recorded carefully
to allow no misreading, the rise to prominence of Leatherwood's spiritual and
political leaders is traced directly to their or their ancestor's serendipitous acquisition of rich swaths of land. Confidently omitting any mythologizing of
the American frontier dream, the novel constructs a model of the "rise to
riches" as a product of blind chance and in some cases as a product of rank
charlatanism. Another example of the novel's cynical reevaluation of more
conventional Howellsian social commentaries, the more wealthy and educated in Leatherwood fall victim to Dylks's promises with little hesitation.
Their acceptance of the theatrics is the harbinger of the entire town's capitu-
lation, and as such it is a commentary on Howells's own frustrated notion that
the key to social reform is the education of the wealthy and powerful. Braile's
historical and literary abstractions cannot overwhelm the desire for easy significations and fail utterly before the promise of salvation "in the flesh," a
clear reference to Freudian self-referentiality. Uneasily enacting the collapse of
Howells's social and literary ideals, a dramatization made more poignant by
its antedating of Howells's own life and projects in the state of his birth, *The
Leatherwood God* represents its author's descent into a disabling irony that
would only be exceeded in scope and cynicism by *The Vacation of the Kelwyns*.

Understood in terms of this cynicism, Howells's remark to Hamlin
Garland that Nancy Billings was the book's "chief figure" becomes both
meaningful and logical. Dylks's former wife, she becomes a bigamist and a
sinner in her own eyes and the eyes of the townspeople the moment Dylks
reappears; her richly textured descriptions stand in stark contrast to the generally Spartan scenes and landscapes in the book: "The figure of a woman who

held her hooded shawl under her chin, stole with the steps often checked through the limp, dew-laden grass of the woods pasture and slipped on the rotting logs . . . she sensed the thick August heat of the sun already smiting its honeyed odors from the corn . . ." (28). Despite Howells's elevation of her, Nancy serves as little more than a conduit for pathos in the text. Victimized by her extreme uncertainty about Dylks and by her sense of loyalty to their son Joey, her primary role in the text seems to be the endurance of suffering and injustice. Her rather frenzied interview of Braile, in the book's eleventh chapter, records her efforts to articulate her personal struggles in theological terms: "A God that would let Joseph Dylks claim to be him, and let them poor fools kneel down to him and worship him? Would an all-wise and all-power-ful God do that? . . . Squire Braile, do you believe that God is good?" (77). Nancy's inquiry—innocent, pathetic, banal—coupled with her quiet refusal to go to the Temple to see Dylks's "miracle" of the seamless raiment, raises her above the townspeople only insofar as she attempts, unlike any other figure in the text, to manage the contradictions around her. She attempts to produce a synthesis of the dialectic represented by Dylks and Braile.

Significantly, it is Nancy's perspective through which the reader watches the procession leading up to the unfulfilled miracle:

> In the August twilight which now began to pale the hot sunset glow, as if she had waited to come alone, in her pride or in her shame, the woman who was bearing the body of the miracle to the place where the wonder was to be wrought, came last of all to pass Nancy where she sat at her door. She was that strong believer who in her utter trust, when she heard that cloth would be needed for the seamless raiment of his miracle, had offered to provide it; and now, neither in pride nor in shame, but in de-fiance of her unbelieving husband, she was bearing away from her house the bolt of linsey-woolsey newly home from the weaver, which was to have been cut into the winter's clothing of her children . . . She carried the bolt wrapped about with her shawl, bearing it tenderly in her arms, as if it were indeed her flesh and blood, her babe which she was going to lay upon an alter of sacrifice. (82)

The image of the cloth as a child, a "babe" to be sacrificed to and for Dylks, suggests to the reader the importance of Nancy's own child, Joey, who in him-self stands as a kind of potential resolution of the text's dialectic. Nancy's care-ful limitation of Joey's exposure to his father and his deep "mysterious" desire to follow Dylks forms a sub-drama within the larger theatrics of Leatherwood. In the family drama, the unmanageable complex of dissent, be-lief, commitment, cynicism, sexuality, and self-denial find resolution in the production of a child. Joey is not a solution, but he is a pragmatic resolution, an emblem of the "salvation in the flesh," the spiritual and physical renewal craved by so many in the town.

Squire Braile's comment, in the final paragraphs of the novel, about "that instinct of maternity," centers the reader's attention on this link between the text's concern with the psychological and the biological. The pathos of Braile's announcement that Nancy, her (second) husband Laban, and their daughter all died of a fever soon after the end of the novel's action serves to further devalue Dylks's struggle with self-deception and Braile's freethinking jurisprudence. At its end, the novel redefines its themes along almost banal lines: no longer interested in competing discourses or theological struggle, when Braile encounters a wandering scholar from Cambridge (Mandeville), he simply describes the Dylks episode as a brief fracturing of family and community. Barely memorable, the tragicomedy of Dylks is perceived as having been one of many scenes in a larger drama of life in the frontier town. Its representation or retelling to the scholar is good porch conversation for Braile, a break from his evening of smoking and calm observation. His manner of rearticulating the events, framed primarily in terms of health and wealth (Nancy's death, Joey's success and general "goodness," the reinforcement through reestablishment of the fractiousness of the town's religious "order") asserts the text's realism by refusing to elevate its material to some high level of significance.

Braile's closing comparison of Dylks to "Joe Smith" who only claimed to be a prophet," while "Dylks claimed to be a god" (159) works toward blocking the easiest and least effective reading of the text. The complexity of the tension in the text between its critique of the believer and its indictment of the "minister" and its exploration of the elaborate cultural theatrics which reinforce such relationships fail utterly if read in the context of a thin polemic against a single belief system or institution. Howells's own lifelong reluctance to produce a "Western" novel, extending from both his autobiographical anxieties and from his annoyance—shared by Clemens—over the "corruption" of the American West, contributed to his desire for some control over the reception of *The Leatherwood God*.[23] Were its themes seen in a "Western" context, they would too easily be dismissed as records of backwoods depravity and the appeal of revivalist rhetoric to the unschooled.

Instead, the text represents Howells's boldest movement away from the "study" or "portraiture" of his earlier novels. Considered largely incomparable to his earlier works, contemporary reviewers and later twentieth-century scholars found a vocabulary for discussing the work in the fiction of Samuel Clemens. Cady concurs, participating in this comparative process and remarking that the Howells of *The Leatherwood God* "is reminiscent of the

Twain of 'The Man that Corrupted Hadleyburg' or *The Mysterious Stranger.*[24]

While it is impossible to argue that Clemens is somehow redrawn through an individual character or complex of characters in *The Leatherwood God,* the connections between the language of Howells's remembrances of him and the development of the novel's themes suggest an active integration of Clemens's personality and aesthetic into Howells's late fiction. It is a peculiar feature of Howells's composition process that he tended to move from inception to published meditation (The "Editor's Study" or "Easy Chair") to the gestation of a novel. His records, so often meticulous, suggest a careful management of his highly productive reputation on one side and a very gradual release of the deeply personal discordance that informed the direction and final shape of his projects. In his final decade of life and composition, 1910–1920, this management of contrasts shifted to a more cynical sense of the irony of a self-actualizing octogenarian largely seen by the press and the marketplace as a known quantity. He wrote on the occasion of his seventieth birthday party in 1907 that the press had made "something of an ado over my birthday in the papers . . . some of the poor fellows in their kindness to me, had robbed their standing obituary notices."[25]

It was this sense of public "death" coupled with the death of close friends and family (Clemens and his wife Elinor within two months of each other in 1910) that provoked in Howells the movement toward a literary aesthetic that was at once self-questioning and complicit with the disintegration of his realism. Witness to his own showmanship, like Braile watching the theatrics of Leatherwood from the safety and stability of his station, Howells no longer worked to reintegrate the competing aspects of his career, psychology, and aesthetic. The professional and the imaginative became for him parts of the same ironic whole. *The Leatherwood God* enacts this uneasy but deliberate reconciliation of the restrained moralist with the vendor of ideas as it manages the irony of a realism that undercuts its own claims to verisimilitude.

Clemens stands in Howells's imagination as a useful example of a resolution of the ironies of American literature and the station of the American writer. Easily appealing to popular taste and whim, "grasping" in his imagination and analysis of the darkest corners of the American character, and highly aware of his own complicity with the systems he ridiculed, Clemens presented Howells with a standard for self-evaluation and comparison. That Howells's deepening cynicism dovetailed with Clemens's own darkening private and public expressions in the early twentieth century only reinforced Howells's sense of connection with the Clemens of *The Mysterious Stranger.* Both writers incorporated the image of the imposter into their art as they sensed a flagging of their own optimism and control over the shape and reception of their expressions.

What Howells's remembrances of Clemens demonstrate is a particular awareness and focus on the latter's theatrical integration of his public and private personas:

> The actor doubled the effect of the author's words; and he was a great actor as well as a great author. He was a most consummate actor, with this difference from other actors, that he was first to know the thoughts and invent the fancies to which his voice and action gave the color of life. Representation is the art of other actors; his art was creative as well as representative; it was nothing at second hand.[26]

This evaluation of Clemens, published in a 1910 preface to a collection of his speeches, positions him firmly in a theatrical context. He is a "consummate actor" both in the sense of highly skilled and all-consuming. Described as a master of creation and representation with the implication that the two are distinct forces in the artistic process, Clemens is also characterized as one who is able to "give the color of life" to his "thoughts and fancies." Howells's remembrance of Clemens affectionately figures him as a literary snake oil salesman, one capable of marketing his own fancies under the label of a probing realism. Adding language of economic exchange, Howells reasserts Clemens's originality while subtly undercutting his methods: "Representation is the art of other actors . . . his art was nothing at second hand."

A year later, evaluating Paine's *Life of Mark Twain* for *Harper's*, Howells takes the author to task for his "naïve" approach to Clemens's theatrical personality: "He was essentially an actor," writes Howells, "that is, a child—that is, a poet—. . . always suffering the emotions he expressed."[27] Recalling Howells's assertion that Clemens was "essentially histrionic," the review identifies a childishness in him, a youthful nature and appeal utterly unavailable to the aging Howells. As it does so, the review also works to align Clemens with the "aesthetic immaturity" that Howells had long before named as the dominant structure of feeling in the American readership. While critics such as Mencken and Brooks would continue to underscore the "effeminacy" of Howells's works, Howells would counter by refiguring the ostensible "masculinization" of American literary culture as a kind of imaginative adolescence, an emotional and psychological dependency on trend and whim fascinated with the heroicizing of the errant self.[28]

Such remembrances suggest a surprising ambivalence toward Clemens in Howells's fiction and memoirs. It is precisely this uncertainty, this dualistic sense of Clemens the friend and Twain the artist that allowed Howells to restructure his own sense of divided self. To identify the same competing forces in another offered him a vocabulary for self reflection, a point through which he could passively examine his own resistance to and complicity with the theatrics of authorship and literary culture.

The Leatherwood God, as a text composed during these transformative years (1910–1915), stands as a record of this interior conversation. While Howells neither paints himself nor Clemens into any single character, the text's dramatic structure and analysis of the force of personality on individual and communal structures of feeling enact a study of those very characteristics that Clemens embodied most boldly.

Despite widespread critical assumptions reinforced by the opinion of friends and family, Howells resisted the imaginative retirement that seemed all but inevitable upon the publication of *The Leatherwood God.* In the book's final months of composition, he expressed in letters and journals an unabashed desire to gild the text in any manner necessary to make it attractive to the naïve reader and the jaded critic simultaneously. He wrote to T.S. Perry on October 19, 1914: "tell m something about religious imposters and false prophets; so that I can give a learned look to the last chapter of my Leatherwood God? I mean, give me their names, so I can find them in the Encyc. Brit."[29] Hardly the words of a writer bent on concealing his flagging mental energies, this request underscores Howells's heightened interest in the theatrics of authorship.

But stronger evidenced still for Howells's interest in wider market appeal and his desire to broaden and intensify the scope of his reception exists in his inquiries to the film industry. Quite unexpected in the manuscripts of an aging author linked at once to the Fireside poets and to the burgeoning modernist movement, Howells engaged in a series of conversations with directors and screenwriters in relation to the promotion and eventual production of a film version of *The Leatherwood God.* Responding to a salutary letter sent in March, 1917 from the editors of *The Century* who received the *Leatherwood God* as a tremendous success ("Your appearance in our magazine has made a wide stir and brought us hearty congratulations from many quarters. We are all of us feeling happy at the very auspicious launching of your latest work"[30]), Howells contacted his protégé Hamlin Garland in July with interest in conversations with the "moving-picture people . . . tell Col. Brady (scenario director for Vitagraph, in Brooklyn) that I shall be glad to have him do my story on the same terms and conditions as he does your stories." Garland had engaged in a series of film projects on his own, and Howells, who had taken to spending afternoons at the movies, considered *The Leatherwood God* particularly well-suited to the medium.

Such interest in new technologies for aesthetic expression and the ensuing widening of popular appeal reassert the importance of *The Leatherwood God* as an example and measure of Howells's imaginative transformation in the last decade of his life. Uneasily working to rearticulate his theories of realism for himself and for his public, Howells's texts manifest an effort to represent a fractured sense of authorial potency, cultural relevance, and literary sophistication through dramatizing the very crisis he himself experienced in those years. Tapping into his sense and memory of the theatrical personality of Samuel Clemens while responding to the new standards for representation established informally by an incipient modernism and film industry, Howells found new form for his highly ironic twentieth-century realist expressions. Setting a freethinking republican rhetoric into dialogue with a delusional false prophet's revivalist discourse opened an imaginative space within which Howells could explore and ironically dismiss the value of language in the education of the American public. His interest in the silent film expresses most elegantly his frustrations with literary culture in general and with his own mounting crisis of representation.

Chapter Five

The Vacation of the Kelwyns, "The Critical Bookstore," and Henry James's "Right of Leaning Back"

By 1905 William Dean Howells had already become a kind of historical artifact in American literary circles, a comic abstraction of his own realism wars and an estranged parent to the very generation of young writers that he continued to sponsor and review. Amid what would seem to be a series of almost desperate attempts to reimagine and reinvent his artistic persona, and under the tremendous pressure of mounting family and personal tragedies (his wife Elinor and dear friend Samuel Clemens would both die in 1910), Howells produced a series of texts that would chronicle not only his flagging faith in his own realism war but also in the public office of literature.

"I am as usual" Howells wrote in 1907, "busy making my gold-brick, without straw, buried in prosperous slavery to a salary and dreaming of some great achievement hereafter, well knowing that if any achievement of mine has greatness it [is] of heretofore."[1] The demands of Howells's "Editor's Easy Chair" column and contract with Harper and Brothers, while providing him with exceptional financial stability, left him little time and energy to engage in larger imaginative projects. He did continue to produce and to add to his "sheaf of novels," but what had been a public crusade for the transformation of literary practice in America in the 1880s and early 1890s had become for the twentieth-century Howells a perplexing memory.

As his confidence in his own potency as an American man of letters waned, Howells's public and social polemics began to collapse into a series of phenomenological studies of the very literary forms and social ideals he had held dear. In the first decade of the twentieth century, he began to allow a bit of "messiness" into his books. Socially dominant but ideologically residual,

Howells could no longer maintain the wall between his literary and business careers: both were transforming. The energies he had for so long worked to separate now mingled to produce more introspective and self-consciously autobiographical texts that in many cases worked toward the depreciation of his own social and aesthetic ideals.

His 1910 *Imaginary Interviews* contains a collection of such pieces from his Easy Chair columns. It is, characteristically, the "chair" itself that speaks in many of these pieces, and not the columnist. Howells increases the narrative distance even more by twisting genres and framing his arguments in dramatically constructed "interviews" and "conversations." The reader is, in short, invited to be amused and confused; only the most thoughtful would take the time to trace the agency of each argument through the many layers of genre, character, and narration.

In one of the text's more transparent moments, a venerable old author named Eugenio gives advice to aspiring writers:

> While we are still young we are aware of an environing and pervading censure, coming from the rivalry, the envy, the generous emulation, the approval, the disapproval, the love, the hate of all those who witness our endeavor. No smallest slip, no slightest defect will be lost upon this censure, equally useful whether sympathetic or antipathetic. But as we grow old we are sensible of a relaxing, a lifting, a withdrawal of the environing and pervading censure. We have become the objects of a compassionate toleration or a contemptuous indifference; it no longer matters greatly to the world whether we do our work well or ill . . . [2]

Eugenio's advice quickly becomes a kind of lament here. The narrative voice, suddenly slipping into a more personal "we" from the third-person mode of earlier paragraphs, allows a degree of connection between the reader and the usually distant Howells. This Howells, masked by Eugenio, sounds less concerned about his own failing creative energies than he is by the far more brutal "compassion" and "indifference" that have replaced "environing and pervading censure." The passage seems at once deeply honest and highly problematic: it suggests an aging Howells craving the censure that motivated and energized him in his youth but unwilling to commit to the kinds of writing needed to "merit" the censure of a twentieth-century readership.

Rather than seek to emulate the young or to appeal to their tastes, Howells internalized his growing sense of artistic irrelevance and produced a series of texts documenting the failure of his literary and social projects. By 1905 the America he saw around him, so dominated and overwhelmed by the residual paradigms of gilded-age capitalism, was utterly impervious to the innocent liberal democratic ideals he had worked to promote through his realistic fiction. *The Vacation of the Kelwyns* and "The Critical Bookstore" survive as the two best examples of the more cynical and self-critical work that Howells produced in the twentieth century. The texts are eulogies for Howellsian realism, not admissions of error or acts of complicity with new aesthetic modes but rather declarations of powerlessness against an intellectual America hopelessly overwhelmed by its own social inequities and failed ideals.

FROM ALTRURIA TO NEW HAMPSHIRE

Howells wrote *The Vacation of the Kelwyns* over a fifteen-year period between 1905 and the year of his death, 1920. Although 175 pages of the text were put into type by Harper and Brothers in 1909, Howells recalled the typescript and cancelled plans for publication, writing to Frederick Duneka that he wanted to "give it a thorough overhauling."[3] The book was published posthumously by Harper and Brothers, possibly in response to the slight rise in interest in Howells's life and works immediately following his death. Criticized as many of his works were for their "trivial themes" and "meek" subjects, Howells's *Kelwyns* was received by those critics who took the time to read it as a nostalgic semi-autobiographical piece in the vein of *New Leaf Mills.* Its years of composition were uncertain, probably even to the Harpers; one contemporary introduced it as "a novel written by William Dean Howells about 1910 but for unannounced reasons not then published."[4] The origins of the project can in fact be traced to 1905 when, during Henry James's visit to America he and Howells had discussed its subject at Kittery Point. James wrote to Howells in 1906: "But what has become of that so true & so droll little beginning you read me (on the tropic day, & I don't speak of it as an aggravation)—about the people in the country lodgings . . . ? I revert to it with appetite."[5]

James's "appetite" for quality fiction from Howells had scarcely been satisfied in the early years of the twentieth century by the latter's devotion to his Altrurian romances, texts which James regarded with little interest. Howells completed *Through the Eye of the Needle* (1907) as he began *The Vacation of the Kelwyns;* perhaps no longer satisfied with the possibility of bringing utopia to America (as he had been in 1893), he sends Americans to the socialist utopia of Altruria in *Needle,* marrying one of his narrators, Mrs. Eveleth Strange, to Aristides Homos. The text is a chronicle of cultural assimilation: each American who lands, purposefully or accidentally, in Altruria ultimately sheds his or her capitalistic tastes and becomes happily acclimated to the sharing of wealth and labor. Perhaps at James's urging, perhaps because of a personal need for renewed subtlety and self-examination, probably stirred by some combination of both, Howells began to develop the opening chapters of *The Vacation of the Kelwyns* in 1905.

The novel, originally titled *Children of the Summer,* takes as its setting an old but bright and spacious home on the outskirts of a Shaker community in the southern New Hampshire of the mid-1870s. Elmer Kelwyn, a Boston professor of "historical sociology," has chosen to rent the house from the Shakers for a single summer in exchange for the household labor of a local farm family, the Kites. The narrative is dominated by the insurmountable conflicts between the customs, manners, and expectations of the Kelwyn family and their rural hosts. It is an experiment in democratic cohabitation, in the possibilities or impossibilities of communication between people of different social classes and origins. For Howells, this experiment and the anxieties it produced dominated his imaginative work (fiction and "Editor's Easy Chair" entries) throughout the final two decades of his life. If interclass communication was impossible, then, in fact, his hopes for realistic fiction as a functional democratic art form were futile.

The shift in mode from *Through the Eye of the Needle* to *Kelwyns* is striking but less noticeable because of the many years that lapsed between the publication of the texts. Juxtaposed, however, the novels reveal Howells's constantly frustrated desire to complete a successful experiment in democratic reform through his fiction. His closest approaches had been the complex psychological portraits he had drawn of such figures as Silas Lapham and Conrad Dryfoos, studies of the individual American and his or her struggles with the nearly insurmountable conflict between the ideals of American liberal democracy and the injustices of late nineteenth-century capitalism. The grand-scale imaginative worlds he created in the Altrurian romances proved insufficient precisely because the fantasy element, the projection of an ideal model for reform, disregarded the grave exigencies of his cultural moment. Howells recognized this failure: to produce Altruria was to violate his own hopes for realism.

Such overreaching projects were perhaps the natural extension of experiments in the pre-Freudian, pre-Jungian dream worlds of such stories as those collected in *Between the Dark and the Daylight* (1907) and *Questionable Shapes* (1903). Visions of "eidolons" (rarely ghosts but rather "realistic ghosts")[6], intense dreams, and unconscious urges populate these stories, but in nearly every case the narratives close with the question of the possibility of shared psychological experience through supernatural means: visions seen by more than one, dreams shared. Howells's craving for a common language, a common human experience that could serve as a conduit for earnest communication manifests itself in these stories through his exploration of the unmapped depths of human psychology. This trend in Howells's fiction began with the death of his daughter Winifred in 1899 (*In the Shadow of a Dream* appeared in 1890) an event that shook him deeply. He wrote to James in the year of her death: "I can conceive of no hate that could have framed a law so dreadful as the law of death . . . I must believe that love did it."[7] This fiction born of personal pain grew for Howells, over two decades, into another potential route toward a democratic literature. Perhaps, he hoped, beneath the bland "world bourgeois" American type that he bemoans in a July 1906 "Editor's Easy Chair" entry, there is a vibrant national psychology, a locus for spiritual and intellectual change irrespective of class or station.

It is in the midst of such simultaneously cross-pollinating and conflicting projects that *The Vacation of the Kelwyns* began its slow growth. Howells's many efforts to heroicize a fiction that would inspire a reader to reconceptualize his or her private moral debt to a nation of common dreams, aspirations, and opportunities collapsed along with his faith in the possibility of a common point of reference for American self-definition. He would never doubt the revolutionary potential of the written word or the institutional value of genteel literature to the cohesion of an upper-class cultural identity, but these interests, embodied for him on one side by Dreiser and Norris and on the other by Henry James, were not *democratic,* as he understood the term.

The charged faith in his own social ideals that Howells had shown when he quoted Emerson's "The American Scholar" in his 1887 "Editor's Study" (" . . . I embrace the common; I sit at the feet of the familiar and the low . . .")[8] had been fractured by the turn of the twentieth century by the very literature that he had so passionately advocated. The triumphant reemergence of Dreiser's *Sister Carrie* in 1907, the broad-based posthumous following of Stephen Crane and Frank Norris, and the flourishing of "natural language" in fiction: these trends, to Howells's eye, worked to reify class distinctions rather than to build on commonalties that would, he had always hoped, lead to inter-class dialogue, communication, and ultimately education. American experience and American literature were fracturing into multiple axes—a trend perhaps inevitable but distressing to Howells. *The Vacation of the Kelwyns* records this distress on several levels, most strikingly through the cynical and ironic tone so unusual in his fiction. The book is set in the 1870s, a time of great potential and great hardship in America; Howells's choice of setting is reminiscent of the same almost desperate return to unity and innocence found in Henry Adams's *Education* and *Mont St. Michel and Chartres.*

A reviewer, writing for *The Nation* on November 3, 1920, sensed the conflict of the novel: "But here is more than farce . . . here is a document upon that pastoral age. Genteel New England, no less than genteel New York, stood on precarious foundations. Democracy menaced it . . . In the half-and-half society of the seventies there was nothing to do but twist and turn and hint and hope."[9] Perhaps characteristically for a writer on the staff of *the Nation,* this reviewer reads the book as an indictment of the American aristocracy of the 1870s, insular and unprepared for the earnest emergence of American democracy. Howells, on the other hand, writes of an 1870s marked by a kind of bewildered centennial hope. The 1876 he reconstructs, in *Kelwyns,* is an historical and cultural moment when democracy—and the potential for equality—is menaced but alive. [10]

Those few twentieth-century critics who have paid attention to *Kelwyns* have found the book surprisingly rich and relatively uncharacteristic of the Howells that James had criticized for his lack of a "grasping imagination." Richard Chase devotes a chapter of his 1957 *The American Novel and its Tradition* to the book, and grudgingly praises it as a departure for Howells from the norm. For him, and for Lionel Trilling who cites the book in *The Liberal Imagination,* Howells succeeds with *Kelwyns* because of his attention to the striking dissonance between the "reality" of America and the "ideal" of America in the 1870s. The two critics read the book as a fine piece of historical fiction, admiring the sensitivity and detail with which Howells captures the exciting ambiguities of life in that ostensibly "pastoral" but anxious age. For Chase, specifically, each character in *Kelwyns* is forced to disassemble a set of cultural and social preconceptions in order to intellectualize and pragmatically manage the messy realities of early-gilded-age America. This is an especially useful reading of the text if cast more widely to include the epoch of the novel's composition (1905–1920) and the changing imagination of its author faced with his own set of disintegrating ideals and preconceptions.[11]

PROFESSOR KELWYN, HENRY JAMES, AND HOWELLS'S "RIGHT OF LEANING BACK"

Howells creates six primary characters in the novel, each developed with equal energy and attention, none favored to the level of protagonist or hero. The first to be introduced is Professor Kelwyn, a man not unlike Howells but not entirely like him:

> [Kelwyn] was really a very well-read and careful scholar in his department of Historical Sociology, with no thought of applying his science to his own life or conduct. In person, he was not tall, but he was very straight;

he carried himself with a sort of unintentional pomp, and walked with short, stiff steps. He was rather dim behind the spectacles he wore; but he was very pleasant when he spoke, and his mind was not as dry as his voice; when pushed to the wall he was capable of a joke . . . (2)[12]

If there are any remarkable similarities between Howells and Kelwyn it is their Welsh heritage and the fact each was "noticeably a gentleman, if not a gentleman by birth" (3). Kelwyn is developed with great care as a serious man, devoted to his work and thoroughly happy in "the well-netted comfort of his study" (5).[13] He has almost no agency to speak of in the opening chapters of the novel; his life is a steady academic routine, broken only occasionally by visits from enthusiastic students. The novel's narrator works to draw Kelwyn with enough detail to clearly illustrate the utter vapidity of his life and projects. "In politics he was a reformer, and he was faithful in a good deal of committee work" (4). His reformism, to be sure, is as empty as his bureaucratic duties. Even his chosen field (Historical Sociology), the narrator reports, is "the driest branch on the tree of knowledge" (3). To Kelwyn's credit, he makes it "one of the most important of the post-graduate courses" at his unnamed university.

For Howells to address Kelwyn's personal ambivalence to his academic field of social studies was probably enough to perk up Henry James's ears. Here was Howells, the architect of Altruria, addressing for once the disjunction between the spirit and the intellect so inevitable in the life of the "free" democratic subject. Kelwyn is the archetypal loafer, a potential agent weighed by the inertia of his position and his comfort in it. At the end of the second chapter Howells offers Kelwyn a moment of potential action, perhaps the only one in the book, but Kelwyn reacts with a stunning mental lethargy. A Shaker Elder arrives at Kelwyn's Boston home hoping to gain access, through Kelwyn, to the ripe young minds of the students. "He had come," writes Howells, "to Kelwyn because of some account he had read of the kind of work he was doing in the university, and had thought he would be pleased, in his quality of lecturer on Historical Sociology, to know something of the historical experiment of the Shakers" (7). Kelwyn is not pleased and is in fact amused by the "sweet innocence" of the Shaker Elder who thought Kelwyn "might make it the theme of a lecture" (7). Unwilling to humor the elder's proposal to "set forth [Shakerism] to such cultivated youth as must attend Kelwyn's lectures," Kelwyn hears only a passing comment about the large, 25-room home available for rent on the edge of the Shakers' property. His solipsistic rejection of the Shaker's proposal, and by extension the rejection of his culture, sets the novel into motion. By the beginning of chapter 3 the reporter/narrator assumes his cynical tone: "When [the Shaker Elder] took his leave he left Kelwyn with the feeling that he regarded his aspiration with a certain cautious disapproval" (10).

The novel and Howells's long struggle with it hinge on this moment of miscommunication between the Elder and Kelwyn. Howells's waning faith in the possibility of social reform in America was largely a function of his frustration with the lack of individual agency and independent thinking among the nation's intellectual and cultural elite. This anxiety stemmed from his sense of personal and national failure during the Haymarket Affair scarcely a decade before. Howells surely felt this sense of the corrupting insularity of American intellectuals even more deeply because of his lack of a college education.[14] Trapped between a generation of political radicals and an aging community of university elites, Howells could not locate an effective vocabulary for communication with either. In *Kelwyns,* rather than cast this anxiety in the harsher light of autobiography, Howells refracts it through a figure whose position and field would virtually mandate an active social conscience—or at least an exacting scientific attention to social inequities—but who rests on his decidedly comfortable laurels.

Through much of the novel Professor Kelwyn is Whitman's epic loafer, lying on the grass and "inviting his soul," if it cares to awaken. Thanks to the Shaker Elder's tolerance and need for rent, the Kelwyns are invited to take the house for the summer and they do accept. In the pages between the offer and the acceptance, however, the Kelwyns begin to form a series of mental images of their vacation-to-come, and they work anxiously to imagine the farm family with whom they are to share the house:

> They talked a great deal of the affair for the next day or two, and they
> somehow transmuted the financial disability of their prospective tenants
> into something physical; they formed the habit of speaking of them as
> 'those poor little people.' (14)

This process of forming "habits of speaking" recurs throughout the text and acts as an agent of ideological reification, a process of changing perception or misperception to an imagined reality.

It was probably not entirely surprising when, on a hot summer 1905 evening in Kittery Point, Maine, Henry James expressed to Howells his admiration for this opening characterization of Kelwyn. Reacting enthusiastically to the ambivalence of Howells's narrator's or "observer's" portrait of the sociologist ambivalent to reform, James would remember the beginning of the novel in several letters to Howells over the following five years. He wrote to Howells in November 1906 that he remembered with "delight . . . the . . .

thing you read me that hot A.M. in your garden-house & the very perspira-
tion of listening to which breaks out on me as I recall it. It was one of your
happiest and most *your* beginnings, I thought, & wish strength to the renewed beat of your wings."[15] For James Howells's experiment in embracing
such ambivalence as a subject for fiction meant new hope for his friend's flagging artistic career. He considered it "most [Howells'] beginning" because it
was an approach to a deeper and decidedly more Jamesian study of the problems of American democracy and the place of the intellectual within it. It was
truest to Howells' own heart—his own crises—and thus was a novel of great
potential power.

James, of course, did not survive to read *The Vacation of the Kelwyns* as
a published text and in fact never read a page of a draft: he simply remembered and relished the sample Howells had read to him. Despite his distance
from the project, his effect on the changing shape of the slowly composed text
is impossible to disregard. James was, without question, the single most important influence on Howells's later imaginative work. Howells would often
acknowledge this fact inside and outside of their correspondence. James had
managed to negotiate a cultural boundary still impenetrable to Howells. The
former was part of an emergent and energetic "sunburst" of modern literary
productivity, a figure who could fill lecture hall after lecture hall during his
1904–5 visit to America with aspiring young writers and scholars (among
them, Van Wyck Brooks) eager to mine his "The Lesson of Balzac" for useful
material. Many early twentieth-century critics would continue to pair
Howells and James; in January, 1903 the *Atlantic Monthly* published an editorial by Harriet Waters Preston who harshly criticized *The Wings of the Dove*
and Howells's *The Kentons* as texts written by authors renowned "in the last
century and ominously near a generation ago."[16]

Howells would, however, acutely feel his artistic inadequacy next to
James throughout the opening years of the twentieth century. While James
certainly admired Howells's business savvy and continued to rely on him for
lucrative advice, the two would not maintain an even exchange of literary
counsel as they had many years before during their walks around Fresh Pond.
Howells understood that James had always hoped for a greater "depth" in his
fiction; the two never touched on questions of skill or intelligence, although
the New Critics who championed James in the mid-twentieth century did use
James's comparative "genius" to justify and frame their deflations of Howells.
Of course, James's fiction was "deeper" than Howells's because of its admission of uncertainty and unresolvable crises into the novel: Howells usually resisted the open-ended narrative, a taste which stirred years of contentious
debate with James.

Each author urged the other to experiment with his own preferred style; Howells complied only a few times, most memorably with his 1886 *The Undiscovered Country*, largely considered a failure, and with a few pieces he produced during his turn-of-the-century flirtation with the occult and the psychological. James, on the other hand, was unwilling and perhaps unable to comply with Howells's (and William James's) occasional calls for a more "direct" or "compact" style. James would often respond to such advice by claiming powerlessness before the scope of his subjects. He wrote to Howells in 1900, " . . . do what I will for compression, I shall not be able to squeeze my subject into 50,000 words . . . It will make, even if it doesn't, for difficulty, still beat me, 70,000–80,000. . . ."[17] It was not unusual for James to lend such agency to his subjects; to allow a given subject its own breadth and depth was, for James, the sincerest gesture toward a "realism" that an author could conceivably make.

The two men exhibit what might be labeled a sibling rivalry, a deeply affectionate and equally competitive attention to each other's lives and works. Because of James's penchant for tossing letters and manuscripts into the fire, we have access to very few of Howells's letters to him. Considering the body of extant material, there is little evidence that Howells ever publicly strayed from his consistent polite flattery of James's work, but there are a number of suggestive omissions and brief comments that open the possibility that he was as dissatisfied with James's art as James was with his. In 1882 Howells wrote that James's "best efforts seem to me those of romance,"[18] and this sentiment lasted until James's death; Howells eulogized him in the incomplete "The American James" as having been "inveterately and intensely French."[19] He wrote to James in July of 1900, "we read you with a touching constancy, and adore your art, with violent exceptions."[20] This affectionate tone characterizes much of the correspondence between the two, more often on Howells's part than on James's. If nothing else, the depth of their life-long friendship prevented the clear expression of their disagreement on the nature of literary realism and the future of the novel. A potentially rich and productive debate between these two very *dissimilar* minds was stifled by their inevitably interlaced personal lives. In short, they liked each other too much to argue.

This palpable affection, most evident in their long correspondence, belies James's and Howells's competitive and often unflattering estimations of each other's art. At this late stage in both men's careers when their attention turned to the possibility of waning powers and insecure legacies, James and Howells saw in each other exaggerated reflections of their own strengths and weaknesses. For James, Howells was a dilute author, an author without the possibility of a productive literary future. It was unwise, James wrote, for

Howells to continue "questioning in detail, at this time of day, that immense 'liked' & likeable state which is the very air your work draws breath in & the very ground it has under its feet." James counseled Howells to do precisely what he had himself feared and avoided:

> Sink luxuriously into your *position,* your immense record of admirable labour & the right of *leaning back,* on your own terms, that crown this as with the wreath of honour & of ease, & you will do what every one concerned wants quite exceedingly to understand you as doing—& as understanding that you *must* do . . . [21]

This advice abruptly contradicts the portrait James had drawn of Howells, only a few years before, as he sketched his plan for the *Ambassadors* for his American publishers. He traces the source of his subject to a comment by a "désorienté elderly American" (presumably Howells) travelling in Europe who pleads with a younger colleague to "[l]ive all you can: it's a mistake not to. It doesn't so much matter what you do—but live . . . Don't, at any rate, make my mistake. Live!"[22] The disparity between James's 1901 and 1904 impressions of Howells do not so much represent a shift in his attitude toward his old friend's career and art but rather a desire, on James's part, to project onto Howells those aspects of his own troubled career that he was unwilling to accept and to own. [23] For Howells the contradictory messages would all too clearly signal James's lack of confidence in recent projects such as *The Kentons* (1902) and *The Son of Royal Langbrirth* (1903). He would certainly not go on to "beat *Lapham*" if his reputation and the quality of his work continued to wane. It is no wonder then, that Professor Kelwyn "sinks into his position" with such luxurious ambivalence, and it is no wonder that James embraced the depiction with such excitement in 1905.

It is almost ironic to consider Kelwyn's disengagement from the social realities of turn-of-the century America as a Jamesian characteristic; to be sure, Kelwyn is no James, but in some sense he is a projection of Howells's own threatening sense that he was becoming just such an insular artist. Writing ostensibly on American standards of "good manners," (of central interest in *Kelwyns*) Howells used his January 1901 "Editor's Easy Chair" column to comment on James's art and methods. "If," writes Howells, "we could imagine the perfume of a flower without the flower, the bouquet of wine without the wine, we should have something of the effect of [James's] fiction." Embedding his commentary, as always, in the mouths of the animated Easy Chair and a generic respondent, Howells reviews James's recent collection of short stories *The Soft Side* with a tone of detached admiration.

He allows a certain amount of criticism, labeling James too "subliminal," but he ultimately returns to the flattery of an admiring friend and reviewer: "In a time when the miasmas of a gross and palpable fable are thick about us, this exquisite air breathes like a memory and a prophecy of days when fiction was and shall be valued for beauty and distinction."

Where is the twentieth-century Howells in this formula? Certainly unwilling to own the highly feminized "exquisite air" of Jamesian prose and yet still holding at arm's length the "gross and palpable" fables of the young naturalists, Howells projects here a literary future that is utterly impossible and surely meaningless. A fiction valued for "beauty and distinction" would hardly include his own best projects, including *Lapham* and *A Hazard of New Fortunes.* Howells's seeming attempt to delete his own contributions to American literary history can best be understood as a reluctant and perhaps despondent admission that James had succeeded by adopting and developing the very tradition of romance that Howells had so strenuously rejected in his realism war. To compliment James's fiction, in a personal letter, was to politely embrace a friend. To do so publicly, for the Howells of 1901, was to admit that he felt imaginatively disarmed as an artist, and most significantly, as a realist.

THE KITES AND THE SHAKERS

Howells's sense of social and aesthetic impotence was surely exacerbated by the 1901 republication of his "Criticism and Fiction" in one of the few completed volumes of his expensive, incomplete, and unpopular "collected works" series.[24] The call-to-arms in that essay, now sometimes ridiculed (as it was by Frank Norris and would be, decades later, by Brooks, Mencken, and Sinclair Lewis, among others)[25], and at best narrowly read, stood as a constant block to Howells's efforts at redirection and redefinition. Howells's reading of Dostoevsky in "Criticism and Fiction" clearly identifies the dominant vector of his poetics during and following the 1890s: "despite [Dostoevsky's] terrible picture of a soul's agony he is hopeful and wholesome, and teaches in every page patience, merciful judgment, humble helpfulness, and that brotherly responsibility, that duty of man to man, from which not even the Americans are emancipated." By choosing Dostoevsky, an author obsessed with the moral and social isolation of man faced the complexities and disillusionment of emerging modernity, Howells points to newer and subtler threats to American social reform. In an age of emergent imperialism, excessive capitalism, and spiritual crises, Howells strove to reposition literature as a pedagogical and emancipatory force.

It can be argued that "Criticism and Fiction" works, somewhat ambivalently, to recapture the social force most often associated with *Uncle Tom's Cabin* while rejecting out-of-hand the sentimentality of little Eva. Although this seems to suggest an impossibly tangled set of goals, Howells cuts the Gordian knot with a relatively simple sentence: "We invite our novelists," he writes, "to concern themselves with the more smiling aspects of life, which are the more American, and to seek the universal in the individual rather than the social interests." Both Howells's critics and his apologists have often become hopelessly trapped in the lackluster imagery of the first half of this sentence. It is, in fact, the second half that contains a key to reading his later works. By suggesting that writers seek the universal in the *individual* rather than the social interests, Howells returns to Emersonian self-reliance and Jeffersonian liberal democracy. According to this model, a good writer could be a teacher and an emancipator; he or she could free a mind from the corrupt paradigms of late nineteenth and early twentieth-century capitalism and emergent imperialism simply by remaining "true to the facts."

Increasingly aware of his own radical departures from this formula (the Altrurian novels being only the most obvious examples) Howells works in *Kelwyns* to depict an intellectual elite hopelessly engaged with "habits of speaking" that have no bearing whatsoever on facts. Kelwyn and his family operate throughout the novel in a discursive mode that it utterly ironic, utterly tangential, never attentive to "the facts" but rather to some idealized version of their perceived reality, some social standard to which their surroundings and experiences must comply, or else, be labeled "impossible" or "irrelevant." The farm family and the Shakers surrounding the house, unexposed to Boston culture, "speak of the thing that is" and constantly frustrate the Kelwyns with their inability to understand suggestion, nuance, and hint.

The fourth chapter contains the best and earliest example of the disjunction between the farmers' manner of speaking and the Kelwyns.' Mr. Kite visits the Kelwyns' Boston home to introduce himself and to make arrangements with the Kelwyns for their stay. Their agreement is simple: The Kelwyns are to spend the summer and pay rent in exchange for the housekeeping, cooking, gardening, and general service of the Kites. The Kites will stay in the lower floor of the house and will be permitted to live in it, rent free, for the remainder of the year after the Kelwyns leave. The arrangement is ideal—in the minds of the Kelwyns—because it suggests a summer of perfect leisure for them with the added benefit of effortless charity for the poor Kites. When Mr. Kite arrives to introduce himself, however, the sight of him inspires Kelwyn with "a deep disgust" (16). Mrs. Kelwyn speaks through the majority of the scene, testing the status of her ideal:

'Oh yes,' she said brightly. 'You can give us light bread, I suppose?'

The man smiled scornfully, and looked round as if taking an invisible spectator into the joke, and said, 'I guess the Woman can make it for you; I never touch it myself. We have hot biscuit.'

'*We* should like hot bread too, now and then,' Mrs. Kelwyn said.

'You can have it every meal, same's we do,' the man said.

'We shouldn't wish to give Mrs. Kite so much trouble," Mrs. Kelwyn remarked . . . 'I suppose she is used to broiling steak, and—'

'Always fry our'n," the man said . . . (17)

Howells capably manages the dialogue here by comically rendering the complete miscommunication between Mrs. Kelwyn and Kite. Her subtlety is completely missed on him, and she can only assume that his direct discourse is absolutely irrelevant to her. Her expectation was, in fact, a monologue, not a dialogue. When the man she had imagined to be a servant punctuates her instructions with comments on his own tastes and expectations, she reacts with hesitation and confusion.

The Kites' use of dialect, not shared by the Shakers, is a staple in Howells's texts from this period. But unique to *Kelwyns* is the interesting effect that exposure to dialect has on the Kelwyn children throughout the book. The Kelwyns' two boys, Francy and Carl, are blank linguistic slates at the beginning of the novel, not yet entirely socialized into their aristocratic New England discursive mode. In her *Language, Race, and Social Class in Howells's America*, Elsa Nettles maps the effect of the Kites' "habits of speaking" on the boys:

> . . . the Kelwyns suffer not only from the terrible cooking of their tenant's wife, Mrs. Kite (whom her husband calls "the Woman"), but also from the readiness of their two sons to emulate the Kites' bad grammar. When the Kelwyn boys announce that the Kites' son Arthur 'has give us the white horse,' their father corrects them, adding to his wife, 'If we stayed here much longer they would not have a grammatical principle uncorrupted.'[26]

Perhaps more interesting than the boys' grammatical slippages is their unwillingness to collaborate with their parents' objection "by principle" to the simple country food and simple presentation of the Kites. They admire, from the beginning, the simple toughness of Arthur (the Kites' son), and constantly express—to their parents' horror—the desire to share in even the most degrading aspects of his life. In one of the book's most carefully crafted scenes, the family sits down to a meal served by the Kites only to be horrified by its raw lack of refinement:

> Mrs. Kelwyn put the pitcher [of milk] to her face mechanically, and then set it down at arm's-length. Her husband silently looked question, and she audibly explained, 'Cowy.' They were helpless against a lack of neatness which gave the odor of the cow's udder to the milk, and Kelwyn thought how promptly they had once dismissed their milkman at home for cowy milk. . . .
>
> . . . 'I want some cowy milk, papa,' Francy whispered; and Carl whispered, too, '*I* want some cowy milk, papa.' (33)

What was "impossible" to the Kelwyn parents was not only tolerable and acceptable but enticing to the boys. Their engagement with country life—though marred by their clear lack of preparedness for its hardships—posits them (again, somewhat comically) as the kinds of readers Howells called for in *Criticism and Fiction*. They are utterly oblivious of social interests, except when reminded forcefully by their parents, and allow themselves an original relation to the world of the Kites. Howells does not let us forget, of course, that Francy and Carl are only present in this rural universe for a summer, and will be removed back to their "parent culture" in short order.

The very fact that the Kelwyns have children, and therefore the possibility of propagating their own world-view and ideology, stands in stark contrast to the crumbling Shaker community that inhabits the margins of the novel. Howells carries on a long American tradition of eulogizing Utopian dreams in *Kelwyns;* here he enacts a radical inversion of Altruria, casting his socialistic utopia in terms of concrete failure rather than abstract, extra-national success. The Shakers, celibate and childless, unable to penetrate the reified and ideological universes of the upper-class cultural elite and its emergent middle-class facsimiles, represent for Howells the perfect emblem of the failure of a highly spiritualized, optimistic, plain-speaking American tradition. Kelwyn admires the Shakers for their "table, so simple, so wholesome, and yet so varied and appetizing," recognizing in himself an anti-modern impulse that longs, abstractly, for the pleasures of a "simpler time." While he is drawn to the Shaker lifestyle spiritually, he is repulsed by it practically. It is "vacation" to him and has little to do with modern life.

During one of his many reveries on the lawn of the house, Kelwyn invites the Shaker Elder Nathaniel to "take a stretch of turf" and converse with him for a while. "It was becoming a habit of theirs when Elder Nathaniel

called for a half-hour of the philosophic converse he loved" (111). On this occasion, the two discuss their strategy for replacing the Kites who have become
"intolerable" to Kelwyn and his wife. Their conversation is central to the text
and is worth quoting at length:

> 'It all seemed very simple in prospect,' Kelwyn went on. 'We had only to
> say, 'You don't do and you must go.''
>
>   'Yee?' The Elder prompted.
>
>   'Of course we expected that it could be arranged so that they should
> lose nothing—'
>
>   'That could be arranged.'
>
>   'But that doesn't seem conclusive or inconclusive as it did in
> prospect. There is something besides their interest to be considered.
> Their natural pride is to be considered, their unnatural self-respect—for
> they have no reason to respect themselves in their failure with us—and
> their real disgrace before the community if we should turn them out.'
>
>   'Yee,' Elder Nathaniel gently acquiesced. He added, sadly, 'Life is not
> very logical, Friend Kelwyn.'
>
>   'No, or else its logic is in the consequences, not in the actions. Of
> course, consequences flow from causes, but the actions that relate the
> consequences to the causes often seem to be of a quality quite different
> from either.'
>
>   'Yee; but it is in them that our individual responsibility lies. We have
> nothing to do with causes or consequences. They seem to belong to
> God.' (112)

Kelwyn's constant intellectualization of his "plight"—his dissatisfaction
with the Kites and his desire to remove them—reflects his need to avoid at
all costs the personalization of any decision he must make. He wishes to
find a balanced relationship of "cause" and "consequence" that will justify
any action that *will be taken,* not by him but by some imagined community of social judges. This attitude fits well within his position as an
"Historical Sociologist," a student not of human relationships that are but
of human relationships that were and perhaps will be. It is the "social interest" to which he turns, and the "individual action" cited by the Shaker
from which he withdraws.

   Finally, it is the Shaker's blind trust in "God" as the manager of cause
and consequence that renders his theory of "individual action" as hollow as
Kelwyn's hope for redemption through a wider social mandate. The drama
enacted by Howells here is not only based in an absurdly banal concern (the
Kelwyns' dissatisfaction with housekeeping) but is played by actors whose
languages and world-views are utterly powerless and whose discourses, both

rooted in impossibly insular ideological systems, can communicate nothing in the end.

It is Kite who best expresses the tragedy of the empty discourse he sees
flying all around him during the Kelwyns' stay. "I don't care about the
talkin,'" he says his to his wife, "It's the doin' I look at . . . Well, it takes all
kinds to make a world. One thing, I'm glad I ain't *their* kind" (100). Virtually
the entire novel is full of "talkin,'" beginning with Kelwyn's failure to respond
to the Shaker Elder's request for a lecture on his community. The text begins
with a failure to act and descends, from that point, into a field of empty arguments on the consequences of inaction.

Read this way, *The Vacation of the Kelwyns* declares the failure of
"Criticism and Fiction" first by enacting none of the essay's literary programs
and then by positing itself as a declaration of the collapse of individual agency
in American society. It is a text that illustrates the absurdity of literature without public office and abandons itself to the free exchange of private, self-in-
terested, discourse. The novel seems all the more hopeless because it is set in
1870s America, a time that Howells must have remembered fondly as an era
of comparative hope. That the book is subtitled "An Idyl of the Middle
Eighteen-Seventies" is, as Richard Chase suggests, rendered deeply ironic by
its steady disassembly of ideals Howells himself had held dear.

THE PROBLEM OF MR. EMERANCE

Howells's own ideals that he had promoted in "Criticism and Fiction" and in
his novels and journalistic pieces in the closing decades of the nineteenth century do not find an advocate in *The Vacation of Kelwyns*. Kelwyn himself represents an unflattering, distorted self-portrait of a Howells disengaged (except
in theory) from a social optimism more fit for the young and the naïve. It is
appropriate then that the novel contains just such a figure: a young, fresh-
faced, thoroughly untested American Scholar named Ellihu Emerance.

If Kelwyn's portrait suggests Howells's sense of personal failure and disengagement, Emerance's works on the one hand to recapture his youthful enthusiasm and on the other to project a future not entirely abandoned to
cynicism. From the moment of his initial description, "clean-shaven," "gentle, with a trace of involuntary authority," with "a thoughtful knot between
his thoughtful eyes" (47), Emerance stands in perfect contrast to Kelwyn's intellectual disengagement from the present. Throughout the novel he reminds
the Kelwyns that he is "on his way to the Centennial," although he never departs, electing instead to stay within the Shaker community at the Kelwyn's
summer home. His origins are mysterious, and his intentions are enigmatic.

He reveals that he was a teacher and still identifies himself with that position, although he "attended a cooking school last winter" (68).

The Kelwyns are ultimately able to decipher Emerance enough to iden-tify him as one who has "risen above his humble beginnings." He was raised on a farm and still identifies with the Kites's lifestyle. He finds the Kelwyns' treatment of the farm family inappropriate and severe, and he steps in to rem-edy the situation himself, using his fluency with both cultures as a bridge be-tween them. He in fact teaches Mrs. Kite new cooking techniques, working with her in the kitchen to prepare a lavish meal of "gems," "omelets," "broiled meat," and various other country delicacies:

> . . . against the glare from the stove the figure of Emerance was silhou-etted in the act of lifting the broiler from the clinging flames of the fat, and then he reappeared with his coat on, and between his hands the platter holding the beafsteak saved from the morning's purchase, and now serving as the chief dish at a meal that almost rose to the dignity of a dinner. (86)

The prospect of a man cooking is alien and perplexing enough to Kelwyn to make him uncomfortable during the preparation of the meal; however, his anxiety lessens as he tastes the food and realizes that "under the regimen of Mrs. Kite [he had] had the sense of sinking lower and lower in [his] own opin-ion" (87). The good food restores his sense of social station.

The comment frustrates Emerance who engages Kelwyn in a philosoph-ical debate by querying, at first politely, "I wonder how much of what we call our personal dignity is really impersonal . . . Whether we are still in the bondage of the old superstition that the things which defile a man are those which happen *to* him rather than those which happen *from* him" (87). Of course, what Emerance evokes here is the question of works vs. grace: his in-terest in such effects of residual Puritanism on the New England character do not end with his debates with Kelwyn. He comments on the life of the farm people later in the book:

> . . . the average life here is good, and it's not affected by the intimate knowledge of evil around it; the sort of knowledge people don't have in towns, and which would be depraving here if it were not guarded by the principles inherited from the past. If Puritanism were false in doctrine . . . as we both think, it was true in life, and it's as true now as ever . . . (227)

By "intimate knowledge of evil" Emerance can only mean "proximity to na-ture;" it is this "evil" that invigorates the old doctrines and makes them "true in life." People in towns, Emerance suggests, have as little access to the realities of nature as Kelwyn does to the raw materials of a refined meal. This kind of detachment from the practical, the basic, and the natural is, he suggests, quite dangerous.

It is at the moment when Emerance begins to suggest the need for change in the present—a move from the theoretical or doctrinal to lived experience—that Kelwyn becomes uncomfortable and works to shut down the discussion. Emerance claims to be "trying to imagine the sort of religious—it isn't the word—spiritual culture which seems to have pretty well gone out of the world, if it was ever much in it, and which once considered the uncultivated on their own ground and not on the ground of their superiors" (88). Kelwyn's responses become at this point short and abrupt; he is not willing to participate in a discussion about "trying to imagine" culture.

After Emerance leaves, Kelwyn seems slightly perplexed and mostly frustrated by the young man's ideas. He intitialy tells his wife that the discussion amounted to "nonsense," but despite himself he continues to ruminate:

> ' . . . I shouldn't say he was a snob, exactly. If you speculate about such intimate things you are in danger of being misunderstood. But I thought his inquiry was rather interesting. I thought there was something in what he said . . . It seemed a sort of survival of the sort of question that vexed Emerson and Lowell in their turn.'
>
> 'But I don't think Emerson and Lowell would have shown that they were ashamed of getting supper," the girl retorted.
>
> 'They were perplexed by their relation to those who got it for them,' Kelwyn insisted.

Emerance's inquiry does not spur Kelwyn to action, but it does force him, if only briefly, to link his present condition with past ideas that he had considered dead. By remarking that Emerance's arguments "seem a sort of survival" of Emerson and Lowell, he enacts an imaginative reengagement with those ideas.

Emerance does not stop with his dinner-table arguments: in the following chapter (15) he visits a local schoolroom and attempts to work his unorthodox pedagogical theories into the lesson. After a brief "scene out of the tragedy of *Rollo*," performed with heroic stiffness by some boys in the class, Emerance steps in with some unabashedly Howellsian advice:

> 'Now boys,' Emerance briskly accosted them,. . . . 'now I want you to think how you could have spoken and acted if you had really been the friend of a man who was going to be put to death tomorrow morning,

and the guard in the prison, who respected and pitied him . . . try it in
the prose that boys talk . . . '

'We couldn't do it . . . Somebody would have to put it in common
talk for us . . . '

'You're quite right, my boy. The fault is with the man who wrote
the piece. He had a bit of nature to express, but he couldn't do it natu-
rally . . . ' (117)

After class, the boys run away mocking Emerance and the teacher says only,
"how very strange" (118). His entrance into the institution of the schoolroom, and his introduction of unorthodox ideas into an already developed
curriculum, render his ostensibly "dignified" pedagogy useless and somewhat
ridiculous. Howells certainly recalls here the problematic reception of his own
realism in the 1870s, 80s, and 90s, but Emerance is by no means drawn as an
heroic ideologue facing a heavy and conservative literary tradition. He is a
stranger in a country classroom mocked by boys.

Despite the fact that Emerance seems to have so many productive ideas,
projects, and intentions, he is ultimately as much a failure as Kelwyn. Howells
projects and refracts his early-twentieth-century self and his younger, more
optimistic self through Kelwyn and Emerance only to have the two images
equally blurred. By the end of the novel, Emerance has enthusiastically chosen to pursue a career as a playwright and actor: "If I didn't love the art of the
theatre I am afraid I shouldn't care for what we call the 'good' it can do. If the
art didn't come first I would rather be a minister. A minister must be an actor,
you know . . . It's merely this: I enjoyed the acting, but first I want to live it.
I want to act in a play of my own" (171). When Emerance receives a letter
from an actor friend suggesting that he will have a chance to do this, he announces that "[my friend] has provided such a magnificent future for me that
all my groping past and hesitating present have been redeemed by him" (234).
This redemption takes the form of total solipsism: Emerance elects to write a
play and to perform in it, creating and engaging with an imaginative world of
his own making, and to enter a closed circle of self-referential language comparable to Kelwyn's. The one flash of optimism in *Kelwyns* is dimmed by the
ineluctable gravity of this egocentrism and social disengagement.

PARTHENOPE BROOK AND CARRIE KELWYN

Howells's handling of society women in *Kelwyns* is marked by the ambivalence of an author at once critical of what he thought to be the "feminization"
of American literary culture and overwhelmingly indebted to his female readership. While the female characters in the novel—specifically Parthenope and

Mrs. Kelwyn—exhibit a strength and agency unknown to the men of the text, their dramatic intensity is thoroughly domesticized. Enacting "the drama of the teacup" so famously attributed to Howellsian prose by Frank Norris, their inevitably microscopic social concerns and their seeming inability to see beyond dinner tables and wedding plans continuously rechannels the discourse of the novel away from "sociological inquiries." This is not to say that Parthenope and Mrs. Kelwyn do not have strong opinions on the state of society:

> 'He despised us,' said Mrs. Kelwyn, very promptly. 'But that doesn't mean that he won't use us well. I have often noticed that in country people, even when they are much smoother than he was, and I have noticed it in working-people of all kinds. They do despise us, and I don't believe they respect anybody but working people, really, though they're so glad to get out of working when they can. They think we're a kind of children, or fools, because we don't know how to do things with our hands, and all the culture in us won't change them. I could see that man's eye taking in your books and manuscripts, and scorning them.' (21)

Mrs. Kelwyn's ability to extract "theory" from the present social conditions she observes exceeds her husband's; he responds to her comment, "I don't know but you're right, Carry," a typical grammatical construction for Kelwyn, an uncertainty but an acceptance based in his own utter lack of engagement. Much of Carrie Kelwyn's anger stems from the fact that she *is* a capable cook and a well-educated, intelligent person. Her possession of the abstraction "culture," something by her own declaration inaccessible to the Kites, is far more important to her than her many skills.

Richard Chase argues that the women of *Kelwyns* participate in a smaller-scale, domestic version of the shedding of social and cultural ideals experienced by the novel's men. He cites, specifically, Parthenope's decision to accept Emerance's proposal as an act of curtailing her strong (by suggestion excessively strong) will.[27] "A man," Parthenope claims, "ought to have one aim and pursue it unswervingly. It musn't be a selfish aim, and it must be a high one. He must want to be of use in the world, and yet he must have a love of the beautiful. He ought to be philanthropical, but not professionally philanthropical; that's rather weakening" (239). Emerance's own admission that he could not realize this ideal, and his plea to Parthenope that she accept him as an "experiment," offers the novel a sentimental conclusion that could only have been, for Howells, a self-conscious concession to the loyal readers whose ideals he had so long worked to satisfy—even at the expense of his own.

At the very end of the novel the Kelwyns move out of the Shaker man-
sion into a smaller (but desirable) stone house not far away. They leave their
complex social relationship with the Kites and elect to spend the remainder of
the summer keeping their own house, preparing their own meals, and re-
claiming their "dignity" by distancing themselves from even the degrading
memory of their proximity to the farmers.[28] Only the boys express regret,
hugging the Kites' son Arthur "who took the embrace as if that type of thing
had never happened to him before" (256). The closing conversation between
Mrs. Kelwyn and her husband captures Howells's ambivalence:

> 'You think I ought to have gone into the kitchen and labored with
> her? Mr. Emerance did that and you saw what it came to.'
> 'Oh yes, you're right. But I wish I had a better conscience in it all. It
> doesn't seem my private debt that troubles me, but my private portion of
> the public debt which we all somehow owe the incapable, the inade-
> quate, the-the—shiftless.'
> 'Oh, very well,' Mrs. Kelwyn said, with the effect of renunciation
> which seldom failed to dismay Kelwyn. 'If you are going to put that in
> your lectures you will lose all your influence.'
> He laughed sadly. 'Then I won't do it. If I can't exert my influence
> without losing it I won't exert it.' That notion pleased him, and now he
> laughed cheerfully.

In this last line Howells's own sense of powerlessness comes through in
Kelwyn's sad then cheerful laugh. It is Mrs. Kelwyn who articulates the argument for him, but he is unable to deflect it and must acknowledge, most pa-
thetically, that she has captured his own ambivalence perfectly. Howells, at this
late point in his career, knows that his position—as James identified it—depends on his continuing to cater to interests that no longer wield cultural authority. Kelwyn's cheerful laugh is Howells's own act of surrender to his public
persona.

SELF-CENSURE IN "THE CRITICAL BOOKSTORE"

In one of the closing scenes of *The Vacation of the Kelwyns*, a local farmer's
wife, Mrs. Allson appears, leading "the youngest of her children that could
walk, in a gingham slip typically washed and ironed, with a remoter following of her uncombed and barefooted brood" (245). She hands Parthenope a
first-edition Cooper, owned by her husband:

> 'It's one,' she explained, with a country confidence in her pronouns, 'that
> his uncle give him, and he wants you should have it, . . . He ain't ever
> read it, and he'd just as lieves you have it as not . . . ' (245)

This gesture stands as another acknowledgement of defeat in *Kelwyns;* although Mrs. Allson and her husband offer Parthenope the book out of sincere gratitude for her compassion for them, they demonstrate utter disinterest in the object itself and recognize that it somehow "belongs" with Parthenope and with her "cultured" middle-class set. Howells had fought for a universalized literary culture, one where access to fiction—and to books themselves—was not limited to the urbane. He had worked to heroicize a fiction of common, recognizable objects and lives. That he closes *Kelwyns* with the image of a book returning to the city unread by its rural caretakers suggests that Howells is declaring the complete failure of hope for a common interclass American literary discourse. That the book returned is by Cooper suggests Howells's belief that another (less romantic) literature may not have been rejected by the Allsons, and may have been read.

By the years of composition of *The Vacation of the Kelwyns*, Howells had become increasingly doubtful that the new shape of the American marketplace could accommodate any literature that could work outside of a closed niche. His hope for seeking the universal in the individual or any analog of his Emersonian-Jeffersonian democratic dream of a heroicized literature of the commonplace would fail before a publishing industry that not only catered to but worked to create insular markets.[29] His 1913 "The Critical Bookstore," a short piece written in the midst of his slow production and reworking of *The Vacation of the Kelwyns* chronicles Howells's sense of his own half-hearted complicity with a literary marketplace that had little patience for his defunct ideals.

The primary figure of the piece, aptly given the archaic and awkward name Erlcort, decides to open a new kind of bookstore in New York City. He calls it a "critical bookstore" because it is designed to cater to "elaborately simple" tastes by selling only books praised by critics and approved by Erlcort himself. It would work "to stem the tide of worthless fiction" and would follow the tastes of "literary authorities" without regard to popular demand. The analogy of Erlcort's enterprise to Howells's problematic relationship to the new literary marketplace is difficult to miss: "[Erlcort] had his own moments of dejection. The interest of the press in his enterprise had flashed through the Sunday issues of a single week, and then flashed out in lasting darkness . . . he could not realize that nothing is so stale as old news, and that no excess of advertising would have relumed those fitful fires."[30]

The project is a failure, and those few successes Elcort does enjoy come about through significant concessions to market demands. The story's richest set of images involve the planning and decoration of the store:

The genius of the place should be a refined hospitality, such as the gentle old codger [Erlcort] had practised with them, and to facilitate this there should be a pair of high-backed settles, one under each window. The book counter should stretch the whole length of the store, and at intervals beside it, against the book-shelving, should be set old-fashioned chairs, but not too old-fashioned. Against the lower book-shelves on a deeper shelf might be stood against the books a few sketches in water-color, or even oil . . . [31]

Erlcort reluctantly gives in to the wishes of a friend and love-interest, Margaret Green, who suggests that he hang small mirrors along the upper shelves:

" . . . what are these little things hung against the partitions of the shelves?"
"Oh—mirrors. Little round ones."
"But why mirrors of any shape?"
"Nothing; only people like to see themselves in a glass of any shape. And when," Margaret added in a burst of candor, "a woman looks up and sees herself with a book in her hand, she will feel so intellectual she will never put it down. She will buy it."[32]

Erlcort agrees to the mirrors, although he refers to them throughout the story as "immoral." Their appeal to the buyers' vanity does prove strong, and on at least one occasion, a female customer buys a book simply on the basis of the reflection she sees.

Howells's choice of the image is interesting in itself, but perhaps more interesting is Erlcort's ambivalence toward the mirrors. His resistance to them is theatrical at best, and his unconvincing complaints underscore his inevitable surrender to the dominance of the current literary marketplace. The mirrors, like the books, reflect the interests of the individual consumer, not the community. This publishing trend predated the recent increase in advertising and marketing efforts. Publishers had begun to assume, as early as the 1870s, that taste had become a matter of individual preference rather than a community standard. *Publisher's Weekly* defined itself during this period as a journal working to "call the attention of particular customers to books likely to serve their taste."[33]

As in *The Vacation of the Kelwyns*, the clear gendering of the self-reflexive buyer/reader in "The Critical Bookstore" underscores both Howells's dependence on his large female readership and his frustration with it. He had written in his 1901 *Heroines of Fiction* that he believed novelists to be "great in proportion to the accuracy and fullness with which they portray women," and his character Fulkerson of *A Hazard of New Fortunes* had, a decade earlier, called for

... a magazine that will go for the woman's fancy every time . . . [not] with recipes for cooking and fashions and personal gossip about authors and society, but real high-tone literature . . . We've got to recognize that women form three-fourths of the reading public in this country . . . [34]

The mirror image in "The Critical Bookstore" represents another self-reflexive moment for Howells as a narrator and author. The woman who looks in the mirror is hardly an idealized subject; she is, in fact, an unflattering representation of Howells's most loyal reader. In *A Hazard of New Fortunes,* Fulkerson saw an opportunity to open and exploit a new market (in the name of respect for women and their needs). In "The Critical Bookstore" Erlcort simply acknowledges that "it was nearly all women who visited" the store. The tone is at once objective and pitiful: the narrative voice surrounds Erlcort with language that emphasizes his misunderstanding of the futility of his enterprise. He pretends to defy the marketplace, but instead appears as an awkward effeminate "old codger" in an increasingly youthful and masculine America, one in which new wealthy authors drive "electric runabouts."

The story closes with a series of relatively absurd images that manifest Howells's frustration and anxiety. Margaret Green returns to the bookstore to find Erlcort frantically censoring magazines with a black paint roller. After having conceded to include "the big four" magazines in his collection, Erlcort decides that they must be held to the same standards as his books. His reason? "[One] could no more tear out the bad and leave the good than [one] could part vice from virtue in human nature." He must cover "the bad" because it cannot be removed. In the midst of this activity, Erlcort suddenly reverses his position and enters into a diatribe against his own project: "What is the Republic of Letters anyway? A vast, benevolent, generous democracy, where one may have what one likes, or a cold oligarchy where he is compelled to take what is good for him? . . . Literature is the whole world . . . Let the multitude have their truck, their rubbish, their rot . . ."[35]

This is precisely what Howells gives the reader at the end of "The Critical Bookstore." The story ends with an absurd kiss between Erlcort and Margaret ("the elderly girl"): "She stared at him, and she was aware she was letting her mouth hang open. While she was trying for some word to close it with he closed it for her." Howells here offers his modern reader a gesture of surrender and concession, and at the same time admits that such a reader will probably neither read nor understand "The Critical Bookstore." The kiss between awkward "elderly children" is all the "truck and rot" he has to offer. His texts can never be a mirror to this new age, and the new generation will never see themselves in his work.

"The Critical Bookstore" and *The Vacation of the Kelwyns* are only samples of a body of self-reflective works of fiction that Howells produced in the twentieth century. "The Critical Bookstore" documents most directly his imaginative helplessness before the new literary marketplace, and *Kelwyns,* more complexly, declares the failure of his youthful hope for a democratic literary form. The aging Howells found himself forced, in the opening years of the twentieth century, to confront his own residual genteel moralism and to acknowledge its ineffectiveness in post-gilded age America. His realism— thoroughly based in a highly moralized faith in the agency of the individual American—was practically unreadable, and ideologically inaccessible, to an America where class consciousness was no longer limited to a well-read gentry as it had been in the 1870s. With the emergence of lower-class solidarity, working-class consciousness, and literatures that responded to and engaged with both, Howells could only "sink, luxuriously into his *position.*"

Relevant Texts

FROM "THE EDITOR'S STUDY," MARCH 1888

I.

"There are few words so sympathetically compliant with a varied need as the word used to conceal the real character of this new department of the *New Monthly.* In almost every dwelling of any pretensions to taste there is nowadays a study, charmingly imagined by the architect and prettily equipped by the domestic powers, where the master of the house lounges away his leisure, scanty or abundant, and nobody apparently studies. From a very early time, or at least from the opening of the present genteel period when the whole race began to put on airs of intellectual refinement, the "study" has been known; and even in the *Book of Snobs* we read of Major Ponto's study, where "the library consisted mostly of spurs, and pots of blacking; and such branches of literary inquiry were discussed as the fate of the calf or the sentence of the pig. This, to be sure, was the study of a country gentleman, and the study of an editor of such a magazine as ours is necessarily somewhat different, though its appointments are equally expressive, we hope, of cultivated pursuits. It is, in any case, not at all the kind of place which the reader, with his mind full of the Grub Street traditions of literature, would fancy—a narrow den at the top of the house, where the occupant, piled about with books and proofs and manuscripts, darkles in a cloud blown from his own cigar. The real editor, before whom contributors tremble, may be something like this in his habitat and environment; but the unreal editor, the airy, elusive abstraction who edits the Study, is quite another character, and is fittingly circumstanced. Heavy rugs silence the foot upon his floor; nothing but the costliest masterpieces gleam from his walls; the best of the old literatures, in a subtly chorded harmony of bindings, make music to the eye from his shelves, and the freshest of the new load his richly carved mahogany table. His vast windows of flawless plate look out upon the confluent waters of the Hudson and the Charles, with expanses, in the middle distance, of the Mississippi, the Great Lakes, and the Golden Gate, and in the background the misty line of the Thames, with reaches of the remoter Seine, and glints of the Tiber's yellow tide. The peaks of the Apennines, dreamily blending with those of the Seirras, form the vanishing point of the delicious perspective; and we need not say that the edifice in which this study luxuriously lurks commands the very best view of the Washington Monument and the two-part front of the national Capitol. As a last secret we will own that the edifice is an American architect's adaptation of a design by the poet Ariosto, who for reasons of economy built himself a very small house in a back street of Ferrara, while he lavished his palaces on the readers of his poetry at no expense to himself; it was originally in the Spanish taste, but the architect has added some touches of the new Renaissance, and has done what he could to impart a colonial flavor to the whole.

In such keeping, the editor of the Study proposes to sit at fine ease, and talk over with this reader—who will always be welcome here—such matters of literary interest as may come up from time to time, whether suggested by the new books of the day or other accidents of literary life. The reader will, of course, not be allowed to interrupt the editor while he is talking; in return the editor will try to keep his temper, and to be as inconclusive as possible. If the reader disagrees with him upon any point, he will be allowed to write to him for publication, when, if the editor can not expose the reader's folly, he will be apt to suppress his letter. It is meant, in other terms, to make the Study a sort of free parliament, but for the presiding officer only; or, a symposium of one.

The editor comes to his place after a silence of some years in this sort, and has a very pretty store of prejudices to indulge and grudges to satisfy, which he will do with as great decency as possible. Their victims will at once know them for prejudices and grudges, and so no great harm will be done; it is impartiality that is to be feared in these matters, and a man who likes or dislikes can never be impartial—though perhaps a woman might. The editor will not deny that in addition to his prejudices and grudges he has some opinions, honest as opinions go, but cherished possibly because he has had no opportunity to exchange them with others. With a reader reduced to silence, the affair of their expression will be very simple; the reader will accept them or not as he likes, and having no chance to reply, will not be argued into them. While the editor's guest, he is invited to look at the same books and consider the same facts with him, and—tacitly, of course—may disable his judgment as much as he will. If he is not content with this, there will always be a vast body of literature not under discussion, and he may turn for relief to that.

II.

If any one, for example, prefers the *History of England,* which Major Ponto had been reading all the morning when he asked Mr. Snob into his study, there is certainly no reason why he must join the editor in turning over the novels which happen for the most part to cumber his table. If himself a novelist, he will probably not care so much for them as for some solider sorts of literature; he will choose almost any history, or biography, or travels, or volume of *memoires pour servir,* which will feed his imagination and afford him material, like so much life; if he is an unsuccessful novelist, he will in this way spare himself the sting of envy, which certain of the books before us might inflict. Yet, if he is not this, if he is a reader who reads novels, and not a reader who writes them, we think he will do himself a pleasure by looking at a few of them with us . . .

FROM "THE MAN OF LETTERS AS A MAN OF BUSINESS"

I

I think that every man ought to work for his living, without exception, and that when he has once avouched his willingness to work, society should provide him with work and warrant him a living. I do not think any man ought to live by an art. A man's art should be his privilege, when he has proven his fitness to exercise it, and has otherwise earned his daily bread; and its results should be free to all. There is an instinctive sense of this, even in the midst of the grotesque confusion of our economic being; people feel that there is something profane, something impious, in taking money for a picture, or a poem, or a statue. Most of all, the artist himself feels this. He puts on a bold front with the world, to be sure, and brazens it out as Business; but he knows very well that there is something false and vulgar in it; and that the work which cannot be truly priced in money cannot be truly paid in money. He can, of course, say that the priest takes money for reading the marriage service, for christening the new-born babe, and for saying the last office for the dead; that the physician sells healing; that justice itself is paid for; and that he is merely a party to the thing that is and must be. He can say that, as the thing is, unless he sells his art he cannot live, that society will leave him to starve if he does not hit its fancy in a picture, or a poem, or a statue; and all this is bitterly true. He is, and he must be, only too glad if there is a market for his wares. Without a market for his wares he must perish, or turn to making something that will sell better than pictures, or poems, or statues. All the same, the sin and the shame remain, and the averted eye sees them still, with its inward vision.

Many will make believe otherwise, but I would rather not make believe otherwise; and in trying to write of Literature as Business I am tempted to begin by saying that Business is the opprobrium of Literature.

II.

Literature is at once the most intimate and the most articulate of the arts. It cannot impart its effect through the senses or the nerves as the other arts can; it is beautiful only through the intelligence; it is the mind speaking to the mind; until it has been put into absolute terms, of an invariable significance, it does not exist at all. It cannot awaken this emotion in one, and that in another; if it fails to express precisely the meaning of the author, if it does not say HIM, it says nothing, and is nothing. So that when a poet has put his heart, much or little, into a poem, and sold it to a magazine, the scandal is greater than when a painter has sold a picture to a patron, or a sculptor has modelled a statue to order. These are artists less articulate and less intimate than the poet; they are more exterior to their work; they are less personally in it; they part with less of themselves in the dicker. It does not change the nature of the case to say that Tennyson and Longfellow and Emerson sold the poems in which they couched the most mystical messages their genius was charged to bear mankind. They submitted to the conditions which none can escape; but that does not justify the conditions, which are none the less the conditions of hucksters because they are imposed upon poets. If it will serve to make my meaning a little clearer we will suppose that a poet has been crossed in love, or has suffered some real sorrow, like the loss of a wife or child. He pours out his broken heart in verse that shall bring tears of sacred sympathy from his readers, and an editor pays him a hundred dollars for the right of bringing his verse to their notice. It is perfectly true that the poem was not written for these dollars, but it is perfectly true that it was sold for them. The poet must use his emotions to pay his provision bills; he has no other means; society does not propose to pay his bills for him. Yet, and at the end of the ends, the unsophisticated witness finds the transaction ridiculous, finds it repulsive, finds it shabby. Somehow he knows that if our huckstering civilization did not at every moment violate the eternal fitness of things, the poet's song would have been given to the world, and the poet would have been cared for by the whole human brotherhood, as any man should be who does the duty that every man owes it.

The instinctive sense of the dishonor which money-purchase does to art is so strong that sometimes a man of letters who can pay his way otherwise refuses pay for his work, as Lord Byron did, for a while, from a noble pride, and as Count Tolstoy has tried to do, from a noble conscience. But

Byron's publisher profited by a generosity which did not reach his readers; and the Countess Tolstoy collects the copyright which her husband foregoes; so that these two eminent instances of protest against business in literature may be said not to have shaken its money basis. I know of no others; but there may be many that I am culpably ignorant of. Still, I doubt if there are enough to affect the fact that Literature is Business as well as Art, and almost as soon. At present business is the only human solidarity; we are all bound together with that chain, whatever interests and tastes and principles separate us, and I feel quite sure that in writing of the Man of Letters as a Man of Business, I shall attract far more readers than I should in writing of him as an Artist. Besides, as an artist he has been done a great deal already; and a commercial state like ours has really more concern in him as a business man. Perhaps it may sometimes be different; I do not believe it will till the conditions are different, and that is a long way off.

III.

In the meantime I confidently appeal to the reader's imagination with the fact that there are several men of letters among us who are such good men of business that they can command a hundred dollars a thousand words for all they write; and at least one woman of letters who gets a hundred and fifty dollars a thousand words. It is easy to write a thousand words a day, and supposing one of these authors to work steadily, it can be seen that his net earnings during the year would come to some such sum as the President of the United States gets for doing far less work of a much more perishable sort. If the man of letters were wholly a business man this is what would happen; he would make his forty or fifty thousand dollars a year, and be able to consort with bank presidents, and railroad officials, and rich tradesmen, and other flowers of our plutocracy on equal terms. But, unfortunately, from a business point of view, he is also an artist, and the very qualities that enable him to delight the public disable him from delighting it uninterruptedly. "No rose blooms right along," as the English boys at Oxford made an American collegian say in a theme which they imagined for him in his national parlance; and the man of letters, as an artist, is apt to have times and seasons when he cannot blossom. Very often it shall happen that his mind will lie fallow between novels or stories for weeks and months at a stretch; when the suggestions of the friendly editor shall fail to fruit in the essays or articles desired; when the muse shall altogether withhold herself, or shall respond only in a feeble dribble of verse which he might sell indeed, but which it would not be good business for him to put on the market. But supposing him to be a very diligent and continuous worker, and so happy as to have fallen on a theme that delights him and bears him along, he may please himself so ill with the result of his labors that he can do nothing less in artistic conscience than destroy a day's work, a week's work, a month's work. I know one man of letters who wrote to-day, and tore up tomorrow for nearly a whole summer. But even if part of the mistaken work may be saved, because it is good work out of place, and not intrinsically bad, the task of reconstruction wants almost as much time as the production; and then, when all seems done, comes the anxious and endless process of revision. These drawbacks reduce the earning capacity of what I may call the high-cost man of letters in such measure that an author whose name is known everywhere, and whose reputation is commensurate with the boundaries of his country, if it does not transcend them, shall have the income, say, of a rising young physician, known to a few people in a subordinate city.

In view of this fact, so humiliating to an author in the presence of a nation of business men like ours, I do not know that I can establish the man of letters in the popular esteem as very much of a business man after all. He must still have a low rank among practical people; and he will be regarded by the great mass of Americans as perhaps a little off, a little funny, a little soft!

Perhaps not; and yet I would rather not have a consensus of public opinion on the question; I think I am more comfortable without it.

IV.

There is this to be said in defence of men of letters on the business side, that literature is still an infant industry with us, and so far from having been protected by our laws it was exposed for ninety years after the foundation of the republic to the vicious competition of stolen goods. It is true that we now have the international copyright law at last, and we can at least begin to forget our shame; but literary property has only forty-two years of life under our unjust statutes, and if it is attacked by robbers the law does not seek out the aggressors and punish them, as it would seek out and punish the trespassers upon any other kind of property; but it leaves the aggrieved owner to bring suit against them, and recover damages, if he can. This may be right enough in itself; but I think, then, that all property should be defended by civil suit, and should become public after forty-two years of private tenure. The Constitution guarantees us all equality before the law, but the law-makers seem to have forgotten this in the case of our infant literary industry. So long as this remains the case, we cannot expect the best business talent to go into literature, and the man of letters must keep his present low grade among business men.

As I have hinted, it is but a little while that he has had any standing at all. I may say that it is only since the was that literature has become a business with us. Before that time we had authors, and very good ones; it is astonishing how good they were; but I do not remember any of them who lived by literature except Edgar A. Poe, perhaps; and we all know how he lived; it was largely upon loans. They were either men of fortune, or they were editors, or professors, with salaries or incomes apart from the small gains of their pens; or they were helped out with public offices; one need not go over their names, or classify them. Some of them must have made money by their books, but I question whether any one could have lived, even very simply, upon the money his books brought him. No one could do that now, unless he wrote a book that we could not recognize as a work of literature. But many authors live now, and live prettily enough, by the sale of the serial publication of their writings to the magazines. They do not live so nicely as successful tradespeople, of course, or as men in the other professions when they begin to make themselves names; the high state of brokers, bankers, railroad operators, and the like is, in the nature of the case, beyond their fondest dreams of pecuniary affluence and social splendor. Perhaps they do not want the chief seats in the synagogue; it is certain they do not get them. Still, they do very fairly well, as things go; and several have incomes that would seem riches to the great mass of worthy Americans who work with their hands for a living—when they can get the work. Their incomes are mainly from serial publication in the different magazines; and the prosperity of the magazines has given a whole class existence which, as a class, was wholly unknown among us before the war. It is not only the famous or fully recognized authors who live in this way, but the much larger number of clever people who are as yet known chiefly to the editors, and who may never make themselves a public, but who do well a kind of acceptable work. These are the sort who do not get reprinted from the periodicals; but the better recognized authors do get reprinted, and then their serial work in its completed form appeals to the readers who say they do not read serials. The multitude of these is not great, and if an author rested his hopes upon their favor he would be a much more embittered man than he now generally is. But he understands perfectly well that his reward is in the serial and not in the book; the return from that he may count as so much money found in the road—a few hundreds, a very few thousands, at the most.

V.

I doubt, indeed, whether the earnings of literary men are absolutely as great as they were earlier in the century, in any of the English-speaking countries; relatively they are nothing like as great. Scott had forty thousand dollars for "Woodstock," which was not a very large novel, and was by no means one of his best; and forty thousand dollars had at least the purchasing powers of sixty thousand then. Moore had three thousand guineas for "Lalla Rookh," but what publisher would be rash enough to pay twenty-five thousand dollars for the masterpiece of a minor poet now? The book, except in very rare instances, makes nothing like the return to the author that the magazine makes, and there are but two or three authors who find their account in that form of publication. Those who do, those who sell the most widely in book form, are often not at all desired by editors; with difficulty they get a serial accepted by any principal magazine. On the other hand, there are authors whose books, compared with those of the popular favorites, do not sell, and yet they are eagerly sought for by editors; they are paid the highest prices, and nothing that they offer is refused. These are literary artists; and it ought to be plain from what I am saying that in belles-lettres, at least, most of the best literature now first sees the light in the magazines, and most of the second best appears first in book form. The old-fashioned people who flatter themselves upon their distinction in not reading magazine fiction, or magazine poetry, make a great mistake, and simply class themselves with the public whose taste is so crude that they cannot enjoy the best. Of course this is true mainly, if not merely, of belles-lettres; history, science, politics, metaphysics, in spite of the many excellent articles and papers in these sorts upon what used to be called various emergent occasions, are still to be found at their best in books. The most monumental example of literature, at once light and good, which has first reached the public in book form is in the different publications of Mark Twain; but Mr. Clemens has of late turned to the magazines too, and now takes their mint mark before he passes into general circulation. All this may change again, but at present the magazines—we have no longer any reviews—form the most direct approach to that part of our reading public which likes the highest things in literary art. Their readers, if we may judge from the quality of the literature they get, are more refined than the book readers in our community; and their taste has no doubt been cultivated by that of the disciplined and experienced editors. So far as I have known these they are men of aesthetic conscience, and of generous sympathy. They have their preferences in the different kinds, and they have their theory of what kind will be most acceptable to their readers; but they exercise their selective function with the wish to give them the best things they can. I do not know one of them—and it has been my good fortune to know them nearly all—who would print a wholly inferior thing for the sake of an inferior class of readers, though they may sometimes decline a good thing because for one reason or another they believe it would not be liked. Still, even this does not often happen; they would rather chance the good thing they doubted of than underrate their readers' judgment.

New writers often suppose themselves rejected because they are unknown; but the unknown man of force and quality is of all others the man whom the editor welcomes to his page. He knows that there is always a danger that the reigning favorite may fail to please; that at any rate, in the order of things, he is passing away, and that if the magazine is not to pass away with the men who have made it, there must be a constant infusion of fresh life. Few editors are such fools and knaves as to let their personal feeling disable their judgment; and the young writer who gets his manuscript back may be sure that it is not because the editor dislikes him, for some reason or no reason. Above all, he can trust me that his contribution has not been passed unread, or has failed of the examination it merits. Editors are not men of infallible judgment, but they do use their judgment, and it is usually good.

The young author who wins recognition in a first-class magazine has achieved a double success, first, with the editor, and then with the best reading public. Many factitious and fallacious literary reputations have been made through books, but very few have been made through the magazines, which are not only the best means of living, but of outliving, with the author; they are both bread and fame to him. If I insist a little upon the high office which this modern form of publication fulfils in the literary world, it is because I am impatient of the antiquated and ignorant prejudice which classes the magazines as ephemeral. They are ephemeral in form, but in substance they are not ephemeral, and what is best in them awaits its resurrection in the book, which, as the first form, is so often a lasting death. An interesting proof of the value of the magazine to literature is the fact that a good novel will have wider acceptance as a book from having been a magazine serial.

I am not sure that the decay of the book is not owing somewhat to the decay of reviewing. This does not now seem to me so thorough, or even so general as it was some years ago, and I think the book oftener comes to the buyer without the warrant of a critical estimate than it once did. That is never the case with material printed in a magazine of high class. A well-trained critic, who is bound by the strongest ties of honor and interest not to betray either his employer or his public, has judged it, and his practical approval is a warrant of quality.

VI.

Under the regime of the great literary periodicals the prosperity of literary men would be much greater than it actually is, if the magazines were altogether literary. But they are not, and this is one reason why literature is still the hungriest of the professions. Two-thirds of the magazines are made up of material which, however excellent, is without literary quality. Very probably this is because even the highest class of readers, who are the magazine readers, have small love of pure literature, which seems to have been growing less and less in all classes. I say seems, because there are really no means of ascertaining the fact, and it may be that the editors are mistaken in making their periodicals two-thirds popular science, politics, economics, and the timely topics which I will call contemporanies; I have sometimes thought they were. But however that may be, their efforts in this direction have narrowed the field of literary industry, and darkened the hope of literary prosperity kindled by the unexampled prosperity of their periodicals. They pay very well indeed for literature; they pay from five or six dollars a thousand words for the work of the unknown writer, to a hundred and fifty dollars a thousand words for that of the most famous, or the most popular, if there is a difference between fame and popularity; but they do not, altogether, want enough literature to justify the best business talent in devoting itself to belles-lettres, to fiction, or poetry, or humorous sketches of travel, or light essays; business talent can do far better in drygoods, groceries, drugs, stocks, real estate, railroads, and the like. I do not think there is any danger of a ruinous competition from it in the field which, though narrow, seems so rich to us poor fellows, whose business talent is small, at the best.

The most of the material contributed to the magazines is the subject of agreement between the editor and the author; it is either suggested by the author, or is the fruit of some suggestion from the editor; in any case the price is stipulated beforehand, and it is no longer the custom for a well-known contributor to leave the payment to the justice or the generosity of the publisher; that was never a fair thing to either, nor ever a wise thing. Usually, the price is so much a thousand words, a truly odious method of computing literary value, and one well calculated to make the author feel keenly the hatefulness of selling his art at all. It is as if a painter sold his picture at so much a square inch, or a sculptor bargained away a group of statuary by the pound. But it is a custom that you cannot always successfully quarrel with, and most writers gladly consent to it, if only the price a thousand words is large enough. The sale to the editor means the sale of the serial rights only, but if the publisher of the magazine is also a publisher of books, the republication of the material is supposed to be his right, unless there is an understanding to the contrary; the terms for this are another affair. Formerly something more could be got for the author by the simultaneous appearance of his work in an English magazine, but now the great American magazines, which pay far higher prices than any others in the world, have a circulation in England so much exceeding that of any English periodical, that the simultaneous publication can no longer be arranged for from this side, though I believe it is still done here from the other side.

VII.

I think this is the case of authorship as it now stands with regard to the magazines. I am not sure that the case is in every way improved for young authors. The magazines all maintain a staff for the careful examination of manuscripts, but as most of the material they print has been engaged, the number of volunteer contributions that they can use is very small; one of the greatest of them, I know, does not use fifty in the course of a year. The new writer, then, must be very good to be accepted, and when accepted he may wait long before he is printed. The pressure is so great in these avenues to the public favor that one, two, three years, are no uncommon periods of delay. If the writer has not the patience for this, or has a soul above cooling his heels in the courts of fame, or must do his best to earn something at once, the book is his immediate hope. How slight a hope the book is I have tried to hint already, but if a book is vulgar enough in sentiment, and crude enough in taste, and flashy enough in incident, or, better or worse still, if it is a bit hot in the mouth, and promises impropriety if not indecency, there is a very fair chance of its success; I do not mean success with a self-respecting publisher, but with the public, which does not personally put its name to it, and is not openly smirched by it. I will not talk of that kind of book, however, but of the book which the young author has written out of an unspoiled heart and an untainted mind, such as most young men and women write; and I will suppose that it has found a publisher. It is human nature, as competition has deformed human nature, for the publisher to wish the author to take all the risks, and he possibly proposes that the author shall publish it at his own expense, and let him have a percentage of the retail price for managing it. If not that, he proposes that the author shall pay for the stereotype plates, and take fifteen per cent. of the price of the book; or if this will not go, if the author cannot, rather than will not do it (he is commonly only too glad to do anything he can), then the publisher offers him ten per cent. of the retail price after the first thousand copies have been sold. But if he fully believes in the book, he will give ten per cent. from the first copy sold, and pay all the costs of publication himself. The book is to be retailed for a dollar and a half, and the publisher is very well pleased with a new book that sells fifteen hundred copies. Whether the author has as much reason to be so is a question, but if the book does not sell more he has only himself to blame, and had better pocket in silence the two hundred and twenty-five dollars he gets for it, and bless his publisher, and try to find work somewhere at five dollars a week. The publisher has not made any more, if quite as much as the author, and until a book has sold two thousand copies the division is fair enough. After that, the heavier expenses of manufacturing have been defrayed, and the book goes on advertising itself; there is merely the cost of paper, printing, binding, and marketing to be met, and the arrangement becomes fairer and fairer for the publisher. The author has no right to complain of this, in the case of his first book, which he is only too grateful to get accepted at all. If it succeeds, he has himself to blame for making the same arrangement for his second or third; it is his fault, or else it is his necessity, which is practically the same thing. It will be business for the publisher to take advantage of his necessity quite the same as if it were his fault; but I do not say that he will always do so; I believe he will very often not do so.

At one time there seemed a probability of the enlargement of the author's gains by subscription publication, and one very well-known American author prospered fabulously in that way. The percentage offered by the subscription houses was only about half as much as that paid by the trade, but the sales were so much greater that the author could very well afford to take it. Where the book-dealer sold ten, the book-agent sold a hundred; or at least he did so in the case of Mark Twain's books; and we all thought it reasonable he could do so with ours. Such of us as made experiment of him, however, found the facts illogical. No book of literary quality was made to go by subscription except Mr. Clemens's books, and I think these went because the subscription public never knew what good literature they were. This sort of readers, or buyers, were so used to getting something worthless for their money, that they would not spend it for artistic fiction, or indeed for any fiction all, except Mr. Clemens's, which they probably supposed bad. Some good books of travel had a measurable success through the book agents, but not at all the success that had been hoped for; and I believe now the subscription trade again publishes only compilations, or such works as owe more to the skill of the editor than the art of the writer. Mr. Clemens himself no longer offers his books to the public in that way.

It is not common, I think, in this country, to publish on the half-profits system, but it is very common in England, where, owing probably to the moisture in the air, which lends a fairy outline to every prospect, it seems to be peculiarly alluring. One of my own early books was published there on these terms, which I accepted with the insensate joy of the young author in getting any terms from a publisher. The book sold, sold every copy of the small first edition, and in due time the publisher's statement came. I did not think my half of the profits was very great, but it seemed a fair division after every imaginable cost had been charged up against my poor book, and that frail venture had been made to pay the expenses of composition, corrections, paper, printing, binding, advertising, and editorial copies. The wonder ought to have been that there was anything at all coming to me, but I was young and greedy then, and I really thought there ought to have been more. I was disappointed, but I made the best of it, of course, and took the account to the junior partner of the house which employed me, and said that I should like to draw on him for the sum due me from the London publishers. He said, Certainly; but after a glance at the account he smiled and said he supposed I knew how much the sum was? I answered, Yes; it was eleven pounds nine shillings, was not it? But I owned at the same time that I never was good at figures, and that I found English money peculiarly baffling. He laughed now, and said, It was eleven shillings and nine pence. In fact, after all those charges for composition, corrections, paper, printing, binding, advertising, and editorial copies, there was a most ingenious and wholly surprising charge of ten per cent. commission on sales, which reduced my half from pounds to shillings, and handsomely increased the publisher's half in proportion. I do not now dispute the justice of the charge. It was not the fault of the half-profits system, it was the fault of the glad young author who did not distinctly inform himself of its mysterious nature in agreeing to it, and had only to reproach himself if he was finally disappointed.

But there is always something disappointing in the accounts of publishers, which I fancy is because authors are strangely constituted, rather than because publishers are so. I will confess that I have such inordinate expectations of the sale of my books which I hope I think modestly of, that the sales reported to me never seem great enough. The copyright due me, no matter how handsome it is, appears deplorably mean, and I feel impoverished for several days after I get it. But then, I ought to add that my balance in the bank is always much less than I have supposed it to be, and my own checks, when they come back to me, have the air of having been in a conspiracy to betray me.

No, we literary men must learn, no matter how we boast ourselves in business, that the distress we feel from our publisher's accounts is simply idiopathic; and I for one wish to bear my witness to the constant good faith and uprightness of publishers.

It is supposed that because they have the affair altogether in their hands they are apt to take advantage in it; but this does not follow, and as a matter of fact they have the affair no more in their own hands than any other business man you have an open account with. There is nothing to prevent you from looking at their books, except your own innermost belief and fear that their books are correct, and that your literature has brought you so little because it has sold so little.

The author is not to blame for his superficial delusion to the contrary, especially if he has written a book that has set everyone talking, because it is of a vital interest. It may be of a vital interest, without being at all the kind of book people want to buy; it may be the kind of book that they are content to know at second hand; there are such fatal books; but hearing so much, and reading so much about it, the author cannot help hoping that it has sold much more than the publisher says. The publisher is undoubtedly honest, however, and the author had better put away the comforting question of his integrity.

The English writers seem largely to suspect their publishers (I cannot say with how much reason, for my English publisher is Scotch, and I should be glad to be so true a man as I think him); but I believe that American authors, when not flown with flattering reviews, as largely trust theirs. Of course there are rogues in every walk of life. I will not say that I ever personally met them in the flowery paths of literature, but I have heard of other people meeting them there, just as I have heard of people seeing ghosts, and I have to believe in both the rogues and the ghosts, without the witness of my own senses. I suppose, upon such grounds mainly, that there are wicked publishers, but in the case of our books that do not sell, I am afraid that it is the graceless and inappreciative public which is far more to blame than the wickedest of the publishers. It is true that publishers will drive a hard bargain when they can, or when they must; but there is nothing to hinder an author from driving a hard bargain, too, when he can, or when he must; and it is to be said of the publisher that he is always more willing to abide by the bargain when it is made than the author is; perhaps because he has the best of it. But he has not always the best of it; I have known publishers too generous to take advantage of the innocence of authors; and I fancy that if publishers had to do with any race less diffident than authors, they would have won a repute for unselfishness that they do not now enjoy. It is certain that in the long period when we flew the black flag of piracy there were many among our corsairs on the high seas of literature who paid a fair price for the stranger craft they seized; still oftener they removed the cargo, and released their capture with several weeks' provision; and although there was undoubtedly a good deal of actual throat-cutting and scuttling, still I feel sure that there was less of it than there would have been in any other line of business released to the unrestricted plunder of the neighbor. There was for a long time even a comity among these amiable buccaneers, who agreed not to interfere with each other, and so were enabled to pay over to their victims some portion of the profit from their stolen goods. Of all business men publishers are probably the most faithful and honorable, and are only surpassed in virtue when men of letters turn business men.

Publishers have their little theories, their little superstitions, and their blind faith in the great god Chance, which we all worship. These things lead them into temptation and adversity, but they seem to do fairly well as business men, even in their own behalf. They do not make above the usual ninety-five per cent. of failures, and more publishers than authors get rich. I have known several publishers who kept their carriages, but I have never known even one author to keep his carriage on the profits of his literature, unless it was in some modest country place where one could take care of one's own horse. But this is simply because the authors are so many, and the publishers are so few. If we wish to reverse their positions, we must study how to reduce the number of authors and increase the number of publishers; then prosperity will smile our way.

VIII.

Some theories or superstitions publishers and authors share together. One of these is that it is best to keep your books all in the hands of one publisher if you can, because then he can give them more attention ad sell more of them. But my own experience is that when my books were in the hands of three publishers they sold quite as well as when one had them; and a fellow author whom I approached in question of this venerable belief, laughed at it. This bold heretic held that it was best to give each new book to a new publisher, for then the fresh man put all his energies into pushing it; but if you had them all together, the publisher rested in a vain security that one book would sell another, and that the fresh venture would revive the public interest in the stale ones. I never knew this to happen, and I must class it with the superstitions of the trade. It may be so in other and more constant countries, but in our fickle republic, each last book has to fight its own way to public favor, much as if it had no sort of literary lineage. Of course this is stating it rather largely, and the truth will be found inside rather than outside of my statement; but there is at least truth enough in it to give the young author pause. While one is preparing to sell his basket of glass, he may as well ask himself whether it is better to part with all to one dealer or not; and if he kicks it over, in spurning the imaginary customer who asks the favor of taking entire stock, that will be his fault, and not the fault of the question.

However, the most important question of all with the man of letters as a man of business, is what kind of book will sell the best of itself, because, at the end of the ends, a book sells itself or does not sell at all; kissing, after long ages of reasoning and a great deal of culture, still goes by favor, and though innumerable generations of horses have been led to water, not one horse has yet been made to drink. With the best, or the worst, will in the world, no publisher can force a book into acceptance. Advertising will not avail, and reviewing is notoriously futile. If the book does not strike the popular fancy, or deal with some universal interest, which need by no means be a profound or important one, the drums and the cymbals shall be beaten in vain. The book may be one of the best and wisest books in the world, but if it has not this sort of appeal in it, the readers of it, and worse yet, the purchasers, will remain few, though fit. The secret of this, like most other secrets of a rather ridiculous world, is in the awful keeping of fate, and we can only hope to surprise it by some lucky chance. To plan a surprise of it, to aim a book at the public favor, is the most hopeless of all endeavors, as it is one of the unworthiest; and I can, neither as a man of letters nor as a man of business, counsel the young author to do it. The best that you can do is to write the book that it gives you the most pleasure to write, to put as much heart and soul as you have about you into it, and then hope as hard as you can to reach the heart and soul of the great multitude of your fellow-men. That, and that alone, is good business for a man of letters.

The failures in literature are no less mystifying than the successes, though they are upon the whole not so mortifying. I have seen a good many of these failures, and I know of one case so signal that I must speak of it, even to the discredit of the public. It is the case of a novelist whose work seems to me of the best that we have done in that sort, whose books represent our life with singular force and singular insight, and whose equipment for his art, through study, travel, and the world, is of the rarest. He has a strong, robust, manly style; his stories are well knit, and his characters are of the flesh and blood complexion which we know in our daily experience; and yet he has failed to achieve one of the first places in our literature; if I named his name here, I am afraid that it would be quite unknown to the greatest part of my readers. I have never been able to account for his want of success, except through the fact that his stories did not please women, though why they did not, I cannot guess. They did not like them for the same reason that they did not like Dr. Fell; and that reason was quite enough for them. It must be enough for him, I am afraid; but I believe that if this author had been writing in a country where men decided the fate of books, the fate of his books would have been different.

The man of letters must make up his mind that in the United States the fate of a book is in the hands of the women. It is the women with us who have the most leisure, and they read the most books. They are far better educated, for the most part, than our men, and their tastes, if not their minds, are more cultivated. Our men read the newspapers, but our women read the books; the more refined among them read the magazines. If they do not always know what is good, they do know what pleases them, and it is useless to quarrel with their decisions, for there is no appeal from them. To go from them to the men

would be going from a higher to a lower court, which would be honestly sur-
prised and bewildered, if the thing were possible. As I say, the author of light
literature, and often the author of solid literature, must resign himself to obscurity unless the ladies choose to recognize him. Yet it would be impossible
to forecast their favor for this kind or that. Who could prophesy it for another,
who guess it for himself? We must strive blindly for it, and hope somehow
that our best will also be our prettiest; but we must remember at the same
time that it is not the ladies' man who is the favorite of the ladies.

There are of course a few, a very few, of our greatest authors, who have
striven forward to the first place in our Valhalla without the help of the largest
reading-class among us; but I should say that these were chiefly the humorists,
for whom women are said nowhere to have any warm liking, and who have
generally with us come up through the newspapers, and have never lost the
favor of the newspaper readers. They have become literary men, as it were,
without the newspapers' readers knowing it; but those who have approached
literature from another direction, have won fame in it chiefly by grace of the
women, who first read them, and then made their husbands and fathers read
them. Perhaps, then, and as a matter of business, it would be well for a serious author, when he finds that he is not pleasing the women, and probably
never will please them, to turn humorous author, and aim at the countenance
of the men. Except as a humorist he certainly never will get it, for your
American, when he is not making money, or trying to do it, is making a joke,
or trying to do it.

IX.

I hope that I have not been hinting that the author who approaches literature
through journalism is not as fine and high a literary man as the author who
comes directly to it, or through some other avenue; I have not the least notion of condemning myself by any such judgment. But I think it is pretty certain that fewer and fewer authors are turning from journalism to literature,
though the entente cordiale between the two professions seems as great as
ever. I fancy, though I may be as mistaken in this as I am in a good many other
things, that most journalists would have been literary men if they could, at the
beginning, and that the kindness they almost always show to young authors
is an effect of the self-pity they feel for their own thwarted wish to be authors.
When an author is once warm in the saddle, and is riding his winged horse to
glory, the case is different: they have then often no sentiment about him; he
is no longer the image of their own young aspiration, and they would will-
ingly see Pegasus buck under him, or have him otherwise brought to grief and
shame. They are apt to gird at him for his unhallowed gains, and they would

be quite right in this if they proposed any way for him to live without them; as I have allowed at the outset, the gains ARE unhallowed. Apparently it is unseemly for an author or two to be making half as much by their pens as popular ministers often receive in salary; the public is used to the pecuniary prosperity of some of the clergy, and at least sees nothing droll in it; but the paragrapher can always get a smile out of his readers at the gross disparity between the ten thousand dollars Jones gets for his novel, and the five pounds Milton got for his epic. I have always thought Milton was paid too little, but I will own that he ought not to have been paid at all, if it comes to that. Again, I say that no man ought to live by any art; it is a shame to the art if not to the artist; but as yet there is no means of the artist's living otherwise, and continuing an artist.

The literary man has certainly no complaint to make of the newspaper man, generally speaking. I have often thought with amazement of the kindness shown by the press to our whole unworthy craft, and of the help so lavishly and freely given to rising and even risen authors. To put it coarsely, brutally, I do not suppose that any other business receives so much gratuitous advertising, except the theatre. It is enormous, the space given in the newspapers to literary notes, literary announcements, reviews, interviews, personal paragraphs, biographies, and all the rest, not to mention the vigorous and incisive attacks made from time to time upon different authors for their opinions of romanticism, realism, capitalism, socialism, Catholicism, and Sandemanianism. I have sometimes doubted whether the public cared for so much of it all as the editors gave them, but I have always said this under my breath, and I have thankfully taken my share of the common bounty. A curious fact, however, is that this vast newspaper publicity seems to have very little to do with an author's popularity, though ever so much with his notoriety. Those strange subterranean fellows who never come to the surface in the newspapers, except for a contemptuous paragraph at long intervals, outsell the famousest of the celebrities, and secretly have their horses and yachts and country seats, while immodest merit is left to get about on foot and look up summer board at the cheaper hotels. That is probably right, or it would not happen; it seems to be in the general scheme, like millionairism and pauperism; but it becomes a question, then, whether the newspapers, with all their friendship for literature, and their actual generosity to literary men, can really help one much to fortune, however much they help one to fame. Such a question is almost too dreadful, and though I have asked it, I will not attempt to answer it. I would much rather consider the question whether if the newspapers can make an author they can also unmake him, and I feel pretty safe in saying that I do not think they can. The Afreet once out of the bottle can never be coaxed back or cudgelled back; and the author whom the newspapers have made cannot be unmade by the newspapers. They consign him to oblivion with a rumor that fills the land, and they keep visiting him there with an uproar which attracts more and more notice to him. An author who has long enjoyed their favor, suddenly and rather mysteriously loses it, through his opinions on certain matters of literary taste, say. For the space of five or six years he is denounced with a unanimity and an incisive vigor that ought to convince him there is something wrong. If he thinks it is his censors, he clings to his opinions with an abiding constance, while ridicule, obloquy, caricature, burlesque, critical refutation and personal detraction follow unsparingly upon every expression, for instance, of his belief that romantic fiction is the highest form of fiction, and that the base, sordid, photographic, commonplace school of Tolstoy, Tourguenief, Zola, Hardy, and James, are unworthy a moment's comparison with the school of Rider Haggard. All this ought certainly to unmake the author in question, and strew his disjecta membra wide over the realm of oblivion. But this is not really the effect. Slowly but surely the clamor dies away, and the author, without relinquishing one of his wicked opinions, or in anywise showing himself repentant, remains apparently whole; and he even returns in a measure to the old kindness: not indeed to the earlier day of perfectly smooth things, but certainly to as much of it as he merits.

I would not have the young author, from this imaginary case, believe that it is well either to court or to defy the good opinion of the press. In fact, it will not only be better taste, but it will be better business for him to keep it altogether out of his mind. There is only one whom he can safely try to please, and that is himself. If he does this he will very probably please other people; but if he does not please himself he may be sure that he will not please them; the book which he has not enjoyed writing, no one will enjoy reading. Still, I would not have him attach too little consequence to the influence of the press. I should say, let him take the celebrity it gives him gratefully but not too seriously; let him reflect that he is often the necessity rather than the ideal of the paragrapher, and that the notoriety the journalists bestow upon him is not the measure of their acquaintance with his work, far less his meaning. They are good fellows, those poor, hard-pushed fellows of the press, but the very conditions of their censure, friendly or unfriendly, forbid it thoroughness, and it must often have more zeal than knowledge in it.

X.

Whether the newspapers will become the rivals of the magazines as the vehicle of literature is a matter that still remains in doubt with the careful observer, after a decade of the newspaper syndicate. Our daily papers never had the habit of the feuilleton as those of the European continent have it; they followed the English tradition in this, though they departed from it in so many other things; and it was not till the Sunday editions of the great dailies arose that there was any real hope for the serial in the papers. I suspect that it was the vast demand for material in their pages—twelve, eighteen, twenty-four, thirty-six—that created the syndicate, for it was the necessity of the Sunday edition not only to have material in abundance, but, with all possible regard for quality, to have it cheap; and the syndicate, when it came into being, imagined a means of meeting this want. It sold the same material to as many newspapers as it could for simultaneous publication in their Sunday editions, which had each its special field, and did not compete with another.

I do not think the syndicate began with serials, and I do not think it is likely to end with them. It has rather worked the vein of interviews, personal adventure, popular science, useful information, travel, sketches, and short stories. Still it has placed a good many serial stories, and at pretty good prices, but not generally so good as those the magazines pay the better sort of writers; for the worse sort it has offered perhaps the best market they have had out of book form. By the newspapers, the syndicate conceives, and perhaps justly, that something sensational is desired; yet all the serial stories it has placed cannot be called sensational. It has enlarged the field of belles-lettres, certainly, but not permanently, I think, in the case of the artistic novel. As yet the women, who form the largest, if not the only cultivated class among us, have not taken very cordially to the Sunday edition, except for its social gossip; they certainly do not go to it for their fiction, and its fiction is mainly of the inferior sort with which boys and men beguile their leisure.

In fact the newspapers prefer to remain newspapers, at least in quality if not in form; and I heard a story the other day from a charming young writer of his experience with them, which may have some instruction for the magazines that less wisely aim to become newspapers. He said that when he carried his work to the editors they struck out what he thought the best of it, because it was what they called magaziny; not contemptuously, but with an instinctive sense of what their readers wanted of them, and did not want. It was apparent that they did not want literary art, or even the appearance of it; they wanted their effects primary; they wanted their emotions raw, or at least saignantes from the joint of fact, and not prepared by the fancy or the taste.

The syndicate has no doubt advanced the prosperity of the short story by increasing the demand for it. We Americans had already done pretty well in that kind, for there was already a great demand for the short story in the magazines; but the syndicate of Sunday editions particularly cultivated it, and made it very paying. I have heard that some short-story writers made the syndicate pay more for their wares than they got from the magazines for them, considering that the magazine publication could enhance their reputation, but the Sunday edition could do nothing for it. They may have been right or not in this; I will not undertake to say, but that was the business view of the case with them.

In spite of the fact that short stories when gathered into a volume and republished would not sell so well as a novel, the short story flourished, and its success in the periodicals began to be felt in the book trade: volumes of short stories suddenly began to sell. But now again, it is said the bottom has dropped out, and they do not sell, and their adversity in book form threatens to affect them in the magazines; an editor told me the other day that he had more short stories than he knew what to do with; and I was not offering him a short story of my own, either.

A permanent decline in the market for a kind of literary art which we have excelled in, or if we have not excelled, have done some of our most exquisite work, would be a pity.

There are other sorts of light literature once greatly in demand, but now apparently no longer desired by editors, who ought to know what their readers desire. Among these is the travel sketch, to me a very agreeable kind, and really to be regretted in its decline. There are some reasons for its decline besides a change of taste in readers, and a possible surfeit. Travel itself has become so universal that everybody, in a manner, has been everywhere, and the foreign scene has no longer the charm of strangeness. We do not think the Old World either so romantic or so ridiculous as we used; and perhaps from an instinctive perception of this altered mood writers no longer appeal to our sentiment or our humor with sketches of outlandish people and places. Of course this can hold true only in a general way; the thing is still done, but not nearly so much done as formerly. When one thinks of the long line of American writers who have greatly pleased in this sort, and who even got their first fame in it, one must grieve to see it obsolescent. Irving, Curtis, Bayard Taylor, Herman Melville, Ross Browne, Ik Marvell, Longfellow, Lowell, Story, Mr. James, Mr. Aldrich, Colonel Hay, Mr. Warner, Mrs. Hunt, Mr. C.W. Stoddard, Mark Twain, and many others whose names will not come to me at the moment, have in their several ways richly contributed to our pleasure in it; but I cannot now fancy a young author finding favor with an editor in a sketch of travel, or a study of foreign manners and customs; his work would have to be of the most signal importance and brilliancy to overcome the editor's feeling that the thing had been done already; and I believe that a publisher if offered a book of such things, would look at it askance, and plead the well-known quiet of the trade. Still, I may be mistaken.

I am rather more confident about the decline of another literary species, namely, the light essay. We have essays enough and to spare, of certain soberer and severer sorts, such as grapple with problems and deal with conditions; but the kind I mean, the slightly humorous, gentle, refined, and humane kind, seems no longer to abound as it once did. I do not know whether the editor discourages them, knowing his readers' frame, or whether they do not offer themselves, but I seldom find them in the magazines. I certainly do not believe that if anyone were now to write essays such as Mr. Warner's "Backlog Studies," an editor would refuse them; and perhaps nobody really writes them. Nobody seems to write the sort that Colonel Higginson formerly contributed to the periodicals, or such as Emerson wrote. Without a great name behind it, I am afraid that a volume of essays would find few buyers, even after the essays had made a public in the magazines. There are, of course, instances to the contrary, but they are not so many or so striking as to make me think that the essay could not be offered as a good opening for business talent.

I suspect that good poetry by well-known hands was never better paid in the magazines than it is now. I must say, too, that I think the quality of the minor poetry of our day is better than that of twenty-five or thirty years ago. I could name half a score of young poets whose work from time to time gives me great pleasure, by the reality of its feeling, and the delicate perfection of its art, but I will not name them, for fear of passing over half a score of others equally meritorious. We have certainly no reason to be discouraged, whatever reason the poets themselves have to be so, and I do not think that even in the short story our younger writers are doing better work than they are doing in the slighter forms of verse. Yet the notion of inviting business talent into this field would be as preposterous as that of asking it to devote itself to the essay. What book of verse by a recent poet, if we except some such peculiarly gifted poet as Mr. Whitcomb Riley, has paid its expenses, not to speak of any profit to the author? Of course, it would be rather more offensive and ridiculous that it should do so than that any other form of literary art should do so; and yet there is no more provision in our economic system for the support of the poet apart from his poems, than there is for the support of the novelist apart from his novel. One could not make any more money by writing poetry than by writing history, but it is a curious fact that while the historians have usually been rich men, and able to afford the luxury of writing history, the poets have usually been poor men, with no pecuniary justification in their devotion to a calling which is so seldom an election.

To be sure, it can be said for them that it costs far less to set up poet than to set up historian. There is no outlay for copying documents, or visiting libraries, or buying books. In fact, except as historian, the man of letters, in whatever walk, has not only none of the expenses of other men of business, but none of the expenses of other artists. He has no such outlay to make for materials, or models, or studio rent as the painter or the sculptor has, and his income, such as it is, is immediate. If he strikes the fancy of the editor with the first thing he offers, as he very well may, it is as well with him as with other men after long years of apprenticeship. Although he will always be the better for an apprenticeship, and the longer apprenticeship the better, he may practically need none at all. Such are the strange conditions of his acceptance with the public, that he may please better without it than with it. An author's first book is too often not only his luckiest, but really his best; it has a brightness that dies out under the school he puts himself to, but a painter or sculptor is only the gainer by all the school he can give himself.

XI.

In view of this fact it become again very hard to establish the author's status in the business world, and at moments I have grave question whether he belongs there at all, except as a novelist. There is, of course, no outlay for him in this sort, any more than in any other sort of literature, but it at least supposes and exacts some measure of preparation. A young writer may produce a brilliant and very perfect romance, just as he may produce a brilliant and very perfect poem, but in the field of realistic fiction, or in what we used to call the novel of manners, a writer can only produce an inferior book at the outset. For this work he needs experience and observation, not so much of others as of himself, for ultimately his characters will all come out of himself, and he will need to know motive and character with such thoroughness and accuracy as he can acquire only through his own heart. A man remains in a measure strange to himself as long as he lives, and the very sources of novelty in his work will be within himself; he can continue to give it freshness in no other way than by knowing himself better and better. But a young writer and an untrained writer has not yet begun to be acquainted even with the lives of other men. The world around him remains a secret as well as the world within him, and both unfold themselves simultaneously to that experience of joy and sorrow that can come only with the lapse of time. Until he is well on toward forty, he will hardly have assimilated the materials of a great novel, although he may have accumulated them. The novelist, then, is a man of letters who is like a man of business in the necessity of preparation for his calling, though he does not pay store-rent, and may carry all his affairs under his hat, as the phrase is. He alone among men of letters may look forward to that sort of continuous prosperity which follows from capacity and diligence in other vocations; for story-telling is now a fairly recognized trade, and the story-teller has a money-standing in the economic world. It is not a very high standing, I think, and I have expressed the belief that it does not bring him the respect felt for men in other lines of business. Still our people cannot deny some consideration to a man who gets a hundred dollars a thousand words. That is a fact appreciable to business, and the man of letters in the line of fiction may reasonably feel that his place in our civilization, though he may owe it to the women who form the great mass of his readers, has something of the character of a vested interest in the eyes of men. There is, indeed, as yet no conspiracy law which will avenge the attempt to injure him in his business. A critic, or a dark conjuration of critics, may damage him at will and to the extent of their power, and he has no recourse but to write better books, or worse. The law will do nothing for him, and a boycott of his books might be preached with immunity by any class of men not liking his opinions on the question of industrial slavery or antipaedobaptism. Still the market for his wares is steadier than the market for any other kind of literary wares, and the prices are better. The historian, who is a kind of inferior realist, has something like the same steadiness in the market, but the prices he can command are much lower, and the two branches of the novelist's trade are not to be compared in a business way. As for the essayist, the poet, the traveller, the popular scientist, they are nowhere in the competition for the favor of readers. The reviewer, indeed, has a pretty steady call for his work, but I fancy the reviewers who get a hundred dollars a thousand words could all stand upon the point of a needle without crowding one another; I should rather like to see them doing it. Another gratifying fact of the situation is that the best writers of fiction who are most in demand with the magazines, probably get nearly as much money for their work as the inferior novelists who outsell them by tens of thousands, and who make their appeal to the innumerable multitude of the less educated and less cultivated buyers of fiction in book-form. I think they earn their money, but if I did not think all of the higher class of novelists earned so much money as they get, I should not be so invidious as to single out for reproach those who did not.

The difficulty about payment, as I have hinted, is that literature has no objective value really, but only a subjective value, if I may so express it. A poem, an essay, a novel, even a paper on political economy, may be worth gold untold to one reader, and worth nothing whatever to another. It may be precious to one mood of the reader, and worthless to another mood of the same reader. How, then, is it to be priced, and how is it to be fairly marketed? All people must be fed, and all people must be clothed, and all people must be housed; and so meat, raiment, and shelter are things of positive and obvious necessity, which may fitly have a market price put upon them. But there is no such positive and obvious necessity, I am sorry to say, for fiction, or not for the higher sort of fiction. The sort of fiction which corresponds to the circus and the variety theatre in the show-business seems essential to the spiritual health of the masses, but the most cultivated of the classes can get on, from time to time, without an artistic novel. This is a great pity, and I should be very willing that readers might feel something like the pangs of hunger and cold, when deprived of their finer fiction; but apparently they never do. Their dumb and passive need is apt only to manifest itself negatively, or in the form of weariness of this author or that. The publisher of books can ascertain the fact through the declining sales of a writer; but the editor of a magazine, who is the best customer of the best writers, must feel the market with a much more delicate touch. Sometimes it may be years before he can satisfy himself that his readers are sick of Smith, and are pining for Jones; even then he cannot know how long their mood will last, and he is by no means safe in cutting down Smith's price and putting up Jones's. With the best will in the world to pay justly, he cannot. Smith, who has been boring his readers to death for a year, may write tomorrow a thing that will please them so much that he will at once be a prime favorite again; and Jones, whom they have been asking for, may do something so uncharacteristic and alien that it will be a flat failure in the magazine. The only thing that gives either writer positive value is his acceptance with the reader; but the acceptance is from month to month wholly uncertain. Authors are largely matters of fashion, like this style of bonnet, or that shape of gown. Last spring the dresses were all made with lace berthas, and Smith was read; this year the butterfly capes are worn, and Jones is the favorite author. Who shall forecast the fall and winter modes?

XII.

In this inquiry it is always the author rather than the publisher, always the contributor rather than the editor, whom I am concerned for. I study the difficulties of the publisher and editor only because they involve the author and the contributor; if they did not, I will not say with how hard a heart I should turn from them; my only pang now in scrutinizing the business conditions of literature is for the makers of literature, not the purveyors of it.

After all, and in spite of my vaunting title, is the man of letters ever a business man? I suppose that, strictly speaking, he never is, except in those rare instances where, through need or choice, he is the publisher as well as the author of his books. Then he puts something on the market and tries to sell it there, and is a man of business. But otherwise he is an artist merely, and is allied to the great mass of wage-workers who are paid for the labor they have put into the thing done or the thing made; who live by doing or making a thing, and not by marketing a thing after some other man has done it or made it. The quality of the thing has nothing to do with the economic nature of the case; the author is, in the last analysis, merely a workingman, and is under the rule that governs the workingman's life. If he is sick or sad, and cannot work, if he is lazy or tipsy and will not, then he earns nothing. He cannot delegate his business to a clerk or a manager; it will not go on while he is sleeping. The wage he can command depends strictly upon his skill and diligence.

I myself am neither sorry nor ashamed for this; I am glad and proud to be of those who eat their bread in the sweat of their own brows, and not the sweat of other men's brows; I think my bread is the sweeter for it. In the mean-time I have no blame for business men; they are no more of the condition of things than we workingmen are; they did no more to cause it or create it; but I would rather be in my place than in theirs, and I wish that I could make all my fellow-artists realize that economically they are the same as mechanics, farmers, day-laborers. It ought to be our glory that we produce something, that we bring into the world something that was not choately there before; that at least we fashion or shape something anew; and we ought to feel the tie that binds us to all the toilers of the shop and field, not as a galling chain, but as a mystic bond also uniting us to Him who works hitherto and evermore.

I know very well that to the vast multitude of our fellow-workingmen we artists are the shadows of names, or not even the shadows. I like to look the facts in the face, for though their lineaments are often terrible, yet there is light nowhere else; and I will not pretend, in this light, that the masses care any more for us than we care for the masses, or so much. Nevertheless, and most distinctly, we are not of the classes. Except in our work, they have no use for us; if now and then they fancy qualifying their material splendor or their spiritual dulness with some artistic presence, the attempt is always a fail-ure that bruises and abashes. In so far as the artist is a man of the world, he is the less an artist, and if he fashions himself upon fashion, he deforms his art. We all know that ghastly type; it is more absurd even than the figure which is really of the world, which was born and bred in it, and conceives of noth-ing outside of it, or above it. In the social world, as well as in the business world, the artist is anomalous, in the actual conditions, and he is perhaps a little ridiculous.

Yet he has to be somewhere, poor fellow, and I think that he will do well to regard himself as in a transition state. He is really of the masses, but they do not know it, and what is worse, they do not know him; as yet the common people do not hear him gladly or hear him at all. He is apparently of the classes; they know him, and they listen to him; he often amuses them very much; but he is not quite at ease among them; whether they know it or not, he knows that he is not of their kind. Perhaps he will never be at home any-where in the world as long as there are masses whom he ought to consort with, and classes whom he cannot consort with. The prospect is not brilliant for any artist now living, but perhaps the artist of the future will see in the flesh the accomplishment of that human equality of which the instinct has been di-vinely planted in the human soul.[1]

Notes

NOTES TO INTRODUCTION

1. William Dean Howells. "Editor's Study." *Harper's New Monthly Magazine* 78(February 1889), 488.
2. "Mr. Howells's Literary Creed." *The Atlantic Monthly.* October, 1891: 566–9.
3. From a description of one of Basil and Isabel March's city walks in *A Hazard of New Fortunes,* New York: Meridian Classic, 1983. p. 259.
4. Donald Pizer, "Crane Reports Garland on Howells," *Modern Language Notes,* LXX (January, 1955): 37–9.
5. See reviews, *The Nation,* July 23, 1891. 390.
6. Hamlin Garland, often considered a protégé of Howells's, would suffer the same disabling relationship to "realism." His attempts to redefine himself and redirect his career coincided with his invention of a new term—"veritism"—which he hoped would constitute an aesthetic blank slate, essentially a fresh start for his young (but faltering) career.
7. Donald Pizer, "Introduction: The Problem of Definition." *The Cambridge Companion to American Realism and Naturalism.* Cambridge, New York: Cambridge University Press, 1995.

NOTES TO PROLOGUE

1. Howells, William Dean. "A Sennight of the Centennial." *The Atlantic Monthly,* July 1876. pg. 103.
2. June 8, 1876. from *Mark Twain-Howells Letters,* 140.
3. See Lillian Miller, 12. Miller offers an interesting comparison between Howells's changing literary tastes and the changing tastes of American artists and art-buyers between the 70s and 80s.

NOTES TO CHAPTER ONE

1. See chapter 4, page 101, for a lengthier discussion of Gosse's comment.

2. In his failed late-1890s collaborative effort with Paul Kester to dramatize *Lapham* for actor James Herne, Howells tolerated a recasting of the ending:

> Walker: Colonel Lapham—a letter from the G. L. & P.
> Rogers: *starting forward as Lapham takes the letter from Walker:* Don't open that letter till you give me your answer—If you break that seal, I wouldn't dare . . .
> *Enter Dinwiddie with telegram in hand.*
> Dinwiddie: We accept your offer to join forces, Colonel Lapham. I've just gotten word from Kanawha. We'd rather go in with you than fight you with more capital.
> Lapham, *stands irresolute. After a pause:* There won't be any fight, Mr. Dinwiddie. (*tears open the envelope.*) I have failed to raise the sum I named. (*Hands letter to Bellingham.*)
> Rogers, *furious. Turns to Ackroyd in despair:* You've ruined me!
> Lapham, *to Bellingham:* I'm in your hands now, Mr. Bellingham, but I'll pay up dollar for dollar. (*He turns to Mrs. Lapham.*) Persis, I want we should go back to Lapham and begin again![1]

As tempting as it may be to excuse Howells from responsibility for this script, manuscript evidence supports the conclusion that he at least supported it if he was not the primary agent in its composition. This excerpt comes from a manuscript written by Kester and incorporates revisions in Howells own hand. It is fair to conclude that he at least did not object to this moral exoneration of Lapham. Whether this represents Howells's desire to revise the novel or to control its reception is uncertain. The Silas in the play is confident and "irresolute" for only an imperceptible stage moment. From Walter J. Meserve, *The Complete Plays of William Dean Howells*. New York: NYU Press, 1960. pp. 481–4.

3. Cited by permission of Houghton Library, Harvard University. James to Howells, bMS Am 1784 (253) 54 January 1888.
4. Howells, "Editor's Study" *Harper's New Monthly Magazine* 78 (February 1889), 488.
5. Bell 32.
6. This paradox would occupy Howells throughout the 1890s and is treated at greatest length in "The Man of Letters as a Man of Business," written in 1892–3, first published in *Scribners* and reprinted in *Literature and Life*, Harper: New York & London, 1902.
7. See above.
8. Noted in Howells's letters from that year; see Howells to James, 25 December 1886: "Our Winny, who's been ailing so long, seems at last to have got her feet on the rising ground again."
9. Anesko, 163.

10. Lynn, 284–6.
11. Sarah Daugherty, "The Realism War as a Campaign that Failed." *American Literary Realism* (29:1), 1997. pg. 22.
12. Cited in Van Wyck Brooks, *Howells, His Life and World.* New York: E.P. Dutton & Company, 1959. pg. 177.
13. Many of Howells's critics offer imprecise accounts of his early readings of Tolstoy. Kenneth Lynn documents his evidence most convincingly, concluding that it was "in the dying months of 1885" that Howells began his systematic readings of Tolstoy (beginning with *The Cossacks*). Lynn writes: "Struggling suddenly, in the dying months of 1885, to break free of his old life, Howells found in Tolstoy's presentation of human suffering the greatest literary inspiration of his lifetime." See Lynn, *William Dean Howells, An American Life.* New York: Harcourt Brace, 1970. pg. 283.
14. Hough, 31.
15. Hough, 32.
16. Howells, "In Honor of Tolstoy," *Critic*, XXX (October, 1898), pg. 288. Also in Howells, *My Literary Passions.* pp. 183–4.
17. The manuscript for *Indian Summer* was completed long before *Lapham* or *Charge*. See J. Henry Harper, *The House of Harper.* New York and London, 1912. pg. 320. For the most complete information on the publication history of *The Minister's Charge*, see the introduction to the University Indiana Library Edition of the text, written by Howard Munford (Nordloh and Kleinmann, eds., *The Minister's Charge*. Bloomington: University of Indiana Press, 1978. pp. xi–xxvi.)
18. Marrion Wilcox, "The Works of William Dean Howells," *Harper's Weekly* 40 (4 July 1896): 655. Michael Anesko also cites and analyzes the comment in *Letters, Fictions, Lives: Henry James and William Dean Howells.* New York, Oxford: Oxford UP, 1997. Pg. 199.
19. Henry James, "William Dean Howells," *Harper's Weekly* 30 (19 June 1886): 394–95.
20. William James would agree with his brother on the merits of *Hazard*, and the book's critical legacy would significantly outshine the line of texts—including *The Minister's Charge, April Hopes,* and *Annie Kilburn*—that preceded it. What represented a "fresh start" to James was, however, an anomaly for Howells, a text, like so many, "that he did not mean to write" produced at a time of significant personal pain.
21. James to Howells, 17 May 1890. Houghton bMS Am 1784 (253) 56.
22. Sewell, Bellingham, and the Coreys, as many of Howells's invented Boston social figures, would recur in his 1880s texts, probably a function of serial publication. A magazine subscriber or purchaser would be more inclined to read a new novel when its episodes offered familiar figures and locales; the work of characterization was therefore much broader and more organic,

comprising Howells's intertextual efforts and the reader's own reception and construction of given figures.

23. A comparison to Howells's description of his own youthful meetings with Longfellow, Lowell, and Holmes in *Years of My Youth* (1916), reveals suggestive similarities, and perhaps more interestingly, anxieties shared by Barker and young Howells about being an unwelcome outsider, an over-reaching boy, and an unworthy pilgrim in a strange land.

24. "Romanticism" narrowly conceived as an idealizing novelistic view of the world.

25. Alan Trachtenberg, *The Incorporation of America, Culture and Society in the Gilded Age*. New York: Hill and Wang, 1982. Pg 185.

26. Trachtenberg, 188.

27. John Seeyle, "The Hole in Howells/The Lapse in *Silas Lapham*." in Donald Pease, ed., *New Essays on the Rise of Silas Lapham*. Cambridge: Cambridge UP, 1991. Pg. 56.

28. John W. Crowley, "*Portrait of a Lady* and *Silas Lapham*." in Donald Pizer, ed., *The Cambridge Companion to American Realism and Naturalism: Howells to London*. Cambridge: Cambridge UP, 1995. Pg. 132.

29. See Anesko, 192–206.

30. Howells to James, 25 December 1886. Cited in Anesko, 259.

31. Cited by permission of Houghton Library, Harvard University. Howells to James, 7 December 1886. Houghton bMS Am 1784 (253) 130.

NOTES TO CHAPTER TWO

1. "Editor's Study." *Harper's Weekly*. January 1888, 154.

2. Cited by permission of Houghton Library, Harvard University. Houghton bMS Am 1094 (242)

3. *A Boy's Town* in *Selected Writings of William Dean Howells*, (ed., Henry Steele Commager. New York: Random House, 1950.) pp. 841–846. See John Crowley, *The Black Heart's Truth: The Early Career of W.D. Howells*. Chapel Hill: UNC Press, 1985, pp. 7–10 for a more lengthy discussion of *A Boy's Town* and Howells's childhood devotion to literature and his "hope of doing something in it."

4. *A Boy's Town*, 843.

5. Howells to James, September 1888.

6. See Cady, *The Realist at War*, 82. Also George Bennet, *The Realism of William Dean Howells: 1889–1920*, Nashville: Vanderbilt UP, 1973. pp. 32–33.

7. Bennet's term, 34.

8. See Clara Marburg Kirk, *William Dean Howells and Art in his Time*, New Brunswick: Rutgers UP, 1965, pg. 193 for a more lengthy discussion of *Annie Kilburn*'s place in the development of Howells's utopian thinking.

9. Again, Clara Marburg Kirk discusses Morris and Howells at length in the chapter "Art and Society," 185–202.
10. Quoted in Kirk, 191–2.
11. William Dean Howells to William Cooper Howells, dated February 2, 1890. *Life in Letters,* II, 1–2.
12. Howells would establish a permanent residence in New York City only in 1891. In 1889 he moved his family back to Boston, to a house on Commonwealth Avenue.
13. *Criticism and Fiction,* 87.
14. Ibid.
15. *The New York Times.* December 15, 1889. pg. 18–19.
16. These comments appear in the "Bibliographical" section—or Howells's prologue—to the 1911 library edition of *A Hazard of New Fortunes* (New York: Harper & Brothers, 1911. pp. v–ix.)
17. Ibid., v.
18. All page references to *A Hazard of New Fortunes* library edition cited above.
19. "On Truth in Fiction," in George Becker, ed., *Documents of Modern Literary Realism.* Princeton: Princeton UP, 1963. pg. 133.
20. Ibid.
21. The December 1889 *New York Times* review of *Hazard* would take Howells's approach to female characters as one of its central subjects. The reviewer argues that Howells "appears to have added to his knowledge of womankind . . . Mrs. March serves as a hyphen between the old type of more or less monotonous unreasonableness and the new type which has a more feminine sense and sensibility." Only two years later in a May 23, 1892 article entitled "Sharp Criticism of Mr. Howells," Ambrose Bierce wrote of Howells shifting "his smug personality and factory of little wooden men and women on wheels to the *Cosmopolitan,* and his following of fibrous virgins, fat matrons, and oleaginous clergymen has probably gone with him to cheer and direct him in pulling down that periodical to the level of inanity from which his successor will have to try to pull up the other." (pg. 5)
22. Howells to James, 10 October 1888.
23. *The Nation,* XLVIII (February 21, 1889: 165–66); *The Critic,* XI (February 9, 1889: 63); *The Literary World,* XX (February 2, 1889: 35).
24. "Editor's Study" *Harper's Magazine,* LXXXI (September, 1890: 639–640).
25. *Criticism and Fiction and Other Essays,* edited by Clara Marburg Kirk and Rudolph Kirk. New York: NYU Press, 1959. p. 346.
26. Cady, *The Realist at War,* 111.
27. Bennet, 42.
28. March's conclusions are all the more suggestive considering Howells's recent loss of his daughter Winny and his own recurring nervous breakdowns.
29. See Bennett, 27.

30. Ibid., 42.
31. Henry Steele Commager, introduction to *The Selected Writings of William Dean Howells*. New York: Random House, 1950. pg. xiii.
32. Gosse, Edmund, "The Limits of Realism in Fiction," *Forum* 9: pp. 391–400, June 1890.

NOTES TO CHAPTER THREE

1. Donald Pizer. "Crane Reports Garland on Howells," *Modern Language Notes,* LXX (January, 1955): 37–39.
2. *Criticism and Fiction,* 15. Quoted in Stanley Corkin, *Realism and the Birth of the Modern United States.* Athens: University of Georgia Press, 1996. pg. 19.
3. The working class consumed dime novels in mass quantities during the mid-late nineteenth century, but these were less of concern to Howells. He worked hardest to educate and persuade the upper classes, hoping for grad-ual, top-down, progressive change.
4. From "The Man of Letters as a Man of Business." Written in 1892–3, first published in *Scribners* and reprinted in *Literature and Life,* Harper: New York & London, 1902.
5. Ballou, 424.
6. J. H. Harper, *The House of Harper.* New York: Harper & Brothers, 1910.
7. Cady, Edwin. *The Realist at War.* Syracuse: Syracuse UP, 1958. pg. 254.
8. See Cady, *The Realist at War,* pages 193–196, for more information on Howells's role in the marketing and design of his own books.
9. Cady, 194.
10. Cady, 195.
11. Cady, 234.
12. See Harper, 318–333, for the full text of a letter submitted by Howells to the author for this history.
13. Excerpted in Harper, 326.
14. Harper, 327.
15. It is easy to forget that in fact during this period all of the New England houses were in some degree of financial trouble. Haper & Brothers was in crisis and undergoing a complete reconstruction and Houghton Mifflin was losing money on its periodicals. All suffered because of the national eco-nomic downturn of the 1890s; it stands to reason that the houses would seek younger, less expensive writers.
16. See Ballou, 463–504.
17. Data from Ballou, 463–480.
18. Ballou, 468.
19. While exclusively contracted with Harpers, if rejected, even temporarily, Howells could, and did, market his materials elsewhere.
20. See Ballou, 481, for these and other related statistics.

21. Cady, 235.
22. See Borus, 219.
23. See Stanley Corkin, 87, for additional details and a more lengthy discussion of Dreiser's appeal to the emergent American imaginative engagement with commercialism and consumerism. Corkin suggests that perhaps *Sister Carrie's* "initial failure was due to Doubleday and Page's lack of marketing initiative, or perhaps it was due to the fact that American readers were not yet used to making the intellectual leaps the book required of them, that is, knowing the meanings of various common objects and being able to apply those meanings directly to objectified humans." Corkin identifies this use of "common objects" as one of the primary differences between Dreiser and Howells; whereas Dreiser embraced the incorporation of America in his texts, Howells relied on "universally recognizable" objects.
24. It was Stephen Crane who seemed poised to inherit and reconstruct Howellsian realism before his death in 1900. Cady and Bell both note that Crane was the Thoreau to Howells's Emerson, the former ready to act on the latter's theories. Crane also had Howells's critical sympathies to an extent Dreiser was never able to claim.
25. Corkin, 86.
26. Corkin, 85.
27. Howells, *Imaginary Interviews*. New York, London: Harper & Brothers, 1910. pg. 297.
28. See Appendix A for samples of these advertising sections.
29. Daniel Borus. *Writing Realism*. Chapel Hill, London: University of North Carolina Press, 1989. pg. 125.
30. Cited in Exman, *The House of Harper*, 192.
31. Exman, 192.
32. See Exman, 190–195
33. *Literature and Life,* xi.
34. ibid, xi.
35. See Bell, 33–38, for a more comprehensive discussion of the links between Howellsian "realism" and the cultural crisis taking place in Boston from 1890–1910. Citing Martin Green's *The Problem of Boston* (1966), Bell examines the conflicting pressures on turn-of-the-century New England writers who, "while seemingly in the most favorable of climates" knew literary life to be "centrally a matter of clubs and sociability."
36. Cited in Bell, 36.
37. Howells, "The Man of Letters as a Man of Business," *Literature and Life,* Pg. 2.
38. *Life in Letters II, 175.*
39. *Life in Letters II,* 349, quoted in Kirk and Kirk, *Howells.* American Book Company: New York, 1950. Pg. 166.
40. from a 1907 letter to S. Weir Mitchell. Cited in Cady, 235.
41. Cady, 235.

42. Howells, *Imaginary Interviews*. New York: Harper & Brothers, 1910. pg. 292.
43. *Imaginary Interviews*, 296.
44. *Imaginary Interviews*, 305.
45. Crowley, 204.
46. *Years of My Youth*. Harper and Brothers: New York, 1916. pg. 226.
47. Early in the war, Howells enthusiastically accepted the seemingly socialistic reforms that the government imposed on the nation, but in letters and journals he becomes increasingly dissatisfied with a government overburdened with bureaucracy and a nation blind to the opportunity for real change.
48. *Youth*, 17.
49. *Youth*, 18.
50. *Youth*, 27.
51. *Youth*, 27.
52. It is not surprising that Brooks reversed his position in 1959 when he was an old man himself; Howells became then for him a great "reporter of America" rather than an old worn-out Bostonian.
53. *Youth*, 124.
54. *Youth*, 227.
55. *Youth*, 159.
56. Cited by permission of Houghton Library, Harvard University. Howells to James, 29 June 1915. Houghton Library, bMS Am 1094 (270).

NOTES TO CHAPTER FOUR

1. Review cited in Thomas Wortham's introduction to *My Mark Twain*, New York: Dover, 1997, pg. xii. *The Nation* reviewed the first book-length version, *My Mark Twain: Reminiscences and Criticisms*, New York: Harper, 1910. See excerpts of revies, Appendix A.
2. Howells to his sister Aurelia, June 21, 1914.
3. All references to *My Mark Twain* refer to the Dover edition cited above.
4. Van Wyck Brooks, *Howells, his Life and World*, New York: E.P. Dutton & Co., 1959. pg 286.
5. See William McMurray, *The Literary Realism of William Dean Howells*, Carbondale: Southern Illinois University Press, 1967, pg. 117.
6. Kirk and Kirk, 198.
7. Cited in Kirk and Kirk, 191.
8. *Selected Mark Twain-Howells Letters,* ed. Frederick Anderson et al., Cambridge: Belknap, 1967, pg. 374. See also Chad Rohman's "Searching for the fructifying dew of truth": "Negative Evidence" and Epistomological Uncertainty in Mark Twain's *No. 44, The Mysterious Stranger*" in *American Literary Realism* 31:2, 1999, pg. 72, for a lengthy discussion of the composition and publication history of *The Mysterious Stranger*, published in the same year as Howells's *Leatherwood God* and vexed by similar autobiographical concerns.

9. he sought information on the Leatherwood Creek episode from his brother Joe in 1904, and remarked that he had received "his very full and satisfactory letter about Leatherwood" on October 14 of that year (in a letter to Aurelia). On November 27, 1904 he wrote to Aurelia that Leatherwood would probably be his next major piece of fiction (*SL 6:114*).

10. This and more comprehensive information on the composition and publication history of *The Leatherwood God* available in Eugene Pattison's introduction to *The Leatherwood God*, Bloomington, London: Indiana University Press, 1976, pp.xi–xxix.

11. All references to *The Leatherwood God* refer to the Indiana University Press Edition.

12. June 21, 1914. *Selected Letters, 1912–1920.*

13. *SL*, 6, 119.

14. On December 7, 1915, Howells wrote to Duneka about the conditions of *The Leatherwood God* publication. *TLG* presented a test case of Howells's new arrangement with Harper & Brothers, which he had explained in his letter to Mildred, 2 November 1915. The Century Company proposed to pay $5,000 for serial use, providing they could publish the novel in book form thereafter, with $1,000 advance against a flat 20% royalty. Harper & Brothers wanted to place the serial elsewhere but keep the novel; but the Century people were insistent on book rights, and Howells signed a contract with them. Howells edited the following comment out of a letter to Duneka (Dec 9, 1915): " . . . You have honestly believed during our relation of fifteen years that I was not serializable, and I do not say that you have been wrong, though I have repeatedly tried to overcome your reluctance." (*SL*)

15. "The Editor's Easy Chair," *Harper's Monthly,* March 1911, cited in Edwin Cady, ed., *W.D. Howells as Critic.* Boston, London: Routledge & Kegan Paul, 1973, pg. 469.

16. February 12, 1913. *Selected Letters, 1912–1920.*

17. August 15, 1913: to Henry James, Jr

18. Harvey cited in John Crowley, *The Dean of American Letters*, Amherst: University of Massachusetts Press, 1999 pg. 101.

19. *Selected Letters 6,* October 28, 1916: Howells to RF Wormwood (editor of Biddeford (ME) *Daily Journal*)

20. Cited in Crowley Jr., 103.

21. Elizabeth Stevens Prioleau, *The Circle of Eros: Sexuality in the Work of William Dean Howells* .Durham: Duke UP, 1983. pg. 179.

22. *North American Review* 175 (September 1902): 293. Also partially cites in Crowley, *The Black Heart's Truth*, 159.

23. See Cady, *The Realist at War*, 264.

24. Ibid, 265.

25. Crowley Jr., 132n.1

26. from George Arms, William M. Gibson, and Frederic C. Marston, Jr. eds., *Prefaces to Contemporaries by William Dean Howells.* Gainesville, FLA: Scholar's Facsimiles & Reprints, 1957, pg 123–124.

27. "Paine's *Life of Mark Twain,*" excerpted in *Selected Literary Criticism* of *William Dean Howells volume III: 1898–1920.* Bloomington: Indiana UP, 1993. 195.

28. Howells's longstanding resistance to this "masculine" literary ideal ironically predicts Hemingway's deification of Twain and his naming of *Huckleberry Finn* as the most important work of nineteenth century American literature.

29. *Selected Letters, v6,* 207.

30. *SL* 6, 240.

NOTES TO CHAPTER FIVE

1. from a 1907 letter to S. Weir Mitchell. Cited in Cady, 235.

2. Howells, *Imaginary Interviews.* New York: Harper & Brothers, 1910. pg. 292.

3. See Michael Anesko, *Letters, Fictions, Lives: Henry James and William Dean Howells.* New York, Oxford: Oxford UP, 1997. n. 10, pg. 433.

4. *The Nation.* v. iii(2887) November 3, 1920.

5. Cited by permission of Houghton Library, Harvard University. James to Howells, 13 September 1906. (Houghton bMS Am 1784 (253) 101).

6. See "The Eidolons of Brooks Alford," 1906.

7. Cited in Michael Anesko, *Letters, Fictions, Lives: Henry James and William Dean Howells.* New York, Oxford: Oxford UP, 1997. pg 201.

8. See Elsa Nettles, *Language, Race, and Social Class in Howells's America.* Lexington: University Press of Kentucky, 1988, pp. 62–71, for a more lengthy discussion of Howells's use of Emerson to develop his own program for realism and dialect.

9. "An Elder America." *The Nation* v.3 (2887) November 3, 1920. pg. 6.

10. On numerous occasions, characters in *The Vacation of the Kelwyns* discuss past and future visits to the "Centennial," presumably the 1876 Centennial Exposition in Philadelphia. These comments date the narrative precisely in the summer of 1876.

11. Chase, like most critics of the novel of his time, announces early in his chapter that *Kelwyns* was written in 1910. Howells did produce a significant part of the novel in that year, but it is impossible to read the novel correctly without taking into account the entire 15-year period of design, composition, editing, rewriting, and finally publication and reception in 1920.

12. All page citations from *The Vacation of the Kelwyns* refer to the 1920 edition, Harper & Brothers.

13. Mosquito netting.

14. By 1905 Howells did have honorary doctorates from Yale, Columbia, and Oxford, but he—like William James—felt acutely his status as an academic outsider.

15. Cited by permission of Houghton Library, Harvard University. James to Howells, 1 November 1906 (Houghton bMS Am 1784 (253) 102)—Anesko 418.

16. Preston's letter is cited in Michael Anesko's *Letters, Fictions, Lives: Henry James and William Dean Howells. Oxford, Oxford UP, 1997. pg. 382.*

17. Cited by permission of Houghton Library, Harvard University. James to Howells, 9 August 1900 (Houghton bMS Am 1784 (253) 75)—Anesko 358.

18. Cited in Van Wyck Brooks. *Howells, His Life and World. New York, E.P. Dutton & Company,* 1959. pg. 219.

19. Anesko, 472.

20. Cited by permission of Houghton Library, Harvard University. Howells to James, 15 July 1900. (Houghton bMS Am 1094 (251)). Anesko, 356.

21. Cited by permission of Houghton Library, Harvard University. James to Howells, 5 August 1904 (Houghton bMS Am 1784 (253) 94)—Anesko 408.

22. From James's ninety-page typescript, "Project of Novel," sent to Harper & Brothers in September 1900. Published in Edel and Powers eds., *The Complete Notebooks of Henry James.* New York, Oxford: Oxford UP, 1987. pp. 542–3.

23. It would be easy—perhaps too easy—to attribute James's changing constructions of Howells to his waxing and waning confidence in his own expatriate status. Rather, Howells represented for him a simplicity and directness of expression that was, in fact, "American" but that ran deeper than national allegiance. The désorienté American of the *Ambassadors* sketch had been driven into reverie by the beauty of a Paris afternoon, while the Howells of the 1904 letter was to embrace the passivity and stillness of an American retirement. The comparison James creates is one of depth vs. surface, life vs. complacency, Jamesian vs. Howellsian realism. It is in fact Howells's prose that James seems to address more than Howells: "The right of leaning back . . . on your own terms" suggests that Howells's established "position" in life and language is poised and stable, without risk. It is American because it is linear, unresponsive to the multivectored uncertainties of life.

24. Howells, William Dean. *Literature and Life.* New York: Harpers, 1901.

25. Van Wyck Brooks would gain a new respect for Howells and his fiction later, in the 1950s, when he wrote with particular enthusiasm about the former's *Indian Summer* (1893).

26. Nettles, 181.

27. See Chase, 180.

28. The similarity to the close of Hawthorne's *House of the Seven Gables* is striking; while there is no extant evidence that Howells had Hawthorne's story in mind, his domesticization of the social reformer and artist will last only until the end of the summer, when the family and the new couple will return to their urbane lives.

29. See Chapter Three (The Market for Realism and American Class-Consciousness)

30. Bardon, Ruth, ed. "The Critical Bookstore." *Selected Short Stories of William Dean Howells.* Athens: Ohio University Press, 1997. pp. 213–214.

31. "The Critical Bookstore," 205.

32. "The Critical Bookstore," 206.

33. Cited in Borus, 39.

34. Cited in John W. Crowley. *The Mask of Fiction—Essays on William Dean Howells.* Amherst: The University of Massachusetts Press, 1989. pg. 40.

35. "The Critical Bookstore," 218.

NOTES TO APPENDIX

1. Original printed in *Scribner's Magazine* 14 (1893), 429–446.

Bibliography

"Mr. Howells's Literary Creed." *The Atlantic Monthly.* October, 1891: 566–9. 1903.

Abbot, Lyman. *Reminiscences.* Boston: Houghton Mifflin, 1915.

Anesko, Michael. *Letters, Fictions, Lives: Henry James and William Dean Howells.* New York, Oxford: Oxford UP, 1997.

Ballou, Ellen. *The Building of the House.* Boston: Houghton Mifflin Company, 1970.

Bardon, Ruth, ed. "The Critical Bookstore." *Selected Short Stories of William Dean Howells.* Athens: Ohio University Press, 1997.

Bardon, Ruth, ed. "The Eidolons of Brooks Alford." *Selected Short Stories of William Dean Howells.* Athens: Ohio University Press, 1997.

Barnett, George E. *The Printers: a Study in American Trade Unionism.* Cambridge: Cambridge UP, 1997.

Bell, Michael D. *The Problem of American Realism.* Chicago: University of Chicago Press, 1993.

Bennet, George. *The Realism of William Dean Howells: 1889–1920,* Nashville: Vanderbilt UP, 1973.

Bennet, George. *William Dean Howells: The Development of a Novelist.* Norman: Univesity of Oklahoma Press, 1973.

Bode, Boyd H. *Modern Education Theories.* New York: Random House/Vintage, 1927.

Bonn, Thomas L. *Under cover: an illustrated history of American mass-market paperbacks.* Harmondsworth, Middlesex, England; New York: Penguin Books, 1982.

Borus, Daniel H. "The Strange Career of American Bohemia." *American Literary History* 14.2 (2002): 376–88.

Borus, Daniel. *Writing Realism: Howells, James, and Norris in the Mass Market.* Chapel Hill, London: University of North Carolina Press, 1989.

British Library. Dept. of Manuscripts, Macmillan, and Co. "Macmillan archives. Publishing records [microform]."

Brooks, Van Wyck. *Howells, His Life and World.* New York: E.P. Dutton & Company, 1959.

Brooks, Van Wyck. *New England: Indian Summer, 1865–1915.* New York: E.P. Dutton, 1941.

Burlingame, Roger. *Endless Frontiers: The Story of McGraw-Hill.* New York: McGraw-Hill Book Company, 1959.

Cady, Edwin H. The Realist At War: The Mature Years 1885–1920 of William Dean Howells. Syracuse: Syracuse UP, 1958.

Clark, Aubert J. *The Movement for International Copyright in Nineteenth-Century America.* Ann Arbor: University Microfilms, 1960.

Commager, Henry Steele, ed. *A Boy's Town* in *Selected Writings of William Dean Howells.* New York: Random House, 1950.

Commager, Henry Steele, introduction to *The Selected Writings of William Dean Howells.* New York: Random House, 1950.

Corkin, Stanley. *Realism and the Birth of the Modern United States.* Athens: University of Georgia Press, 1996.

Crane, E.M. *A Century of Book Publishing.* New York: D. Van Nostrand Company, Inc., 1948.

Crowley, John W. "*Portrait of a Lady* and *Silas Lapham.*" in Donald Pizer, ed., *The Cambridge Companion to American Realism and Naturalism: Howells to London.* Cambridge: Cambridge UP, 1995.

Crowley, John W. *The Mask of Fiction—Essays on William Dean Howells.* Amherst: The University of Massachusetts Press, 1989.

Crowley, John W. *The Black Heart's Truth: The Early Career of W.D. Howells.* Chapel Hill: UNC Press, 1985.

Daugherty, Sarah. "The Realism War as a Campaign that Failed." *American Literary Realism* (29:1), 1997. pg. 19–27.

Daugherty, Sarah B. "'The Home-Towners': Howells the Critic Vs. Howells the Novelist." *American Literary Realism* 34.1 (2001): 66–72.

Davis, Scott Christopher. "Telling Tales: Ideology and the American Observer, 1890–1896." U of California Santa Barbara, 2001.

Dzwonkoski, Peter. *American literary publishing houses, 1638–1899.* Dictionary of literary biography; v. 49. Detroit, Mich.: Gale Research Co., 1986.

Dzwonkoski, Peter. *American literary publishing houses, 1900–1980. Trade and paperback.* Dictionary of literary biography; v. 46. Detroit, Mich.: Gale Research Co., 1986.

Edel, Leon and Powers eds., *The Complete Notebooks of Henry James.* New York, Oxford: Oxford UP, 1987.

Engeman, Thomas S. "Religion and Politics the American way: The Exemplary William Dean Howells." *The Review of Politics,* Notre Dame; Winter 2001; Vol. 63, Iss. 1; pg. 107, 22 pgs.

Exman, Eugene. *The House of Harper.* New York: Harper & Row, 1967.

Ford, James L. *Forty-Odd Years in the Literary Shop.* New York: E.P. Dutton & Company, 1921.

Gosse, Edmund, "The Limits of Realism in Fiction," *Forum* 9: pp. 391–400, June 1890.

Grannis, Chandler B. *What Happens in Book Publishing.* New York: Columbia University Press, 1957.

Gross, Gerald. *Publishers on Publishing.* New York: R.R. Bowker Company, 1961.

Handa, Sangeeta. *Realism in American Fiction : Contribution of William Dean Howells.* Jaipur: Rawat Publications, 2001.

Harper, and Brothers. *Archives of Harper & Brothers, 1817–1914 [microform].* Cambridge[Cambridgeshire]: Chadwyck-Healy; Teaneck, 1980.

Harper, J. Henry. *The House of Harper.* New York: Harper & Brothers, 1912.

Howard, June, foreword. *The Whole Family: A Novel by Twelve Authors.* Durham, NC: Duke UP, 2001.

Howard, June. *Publishing the Family.* New Americanists. Durham, NC: Duke UP, 2001.

Houghton, Mifflin, & Company. *A Portrait Catalogue of the Books Published by Houghton, Mifflin and Company with a Sketch of the Firm, Brief Descriptions of the Various Departments, and Some Account of the Origin and Character of the Literary Enterprises Undertaken.* Boston: Houghton, Mifflin and Company, 1906.

Howe, M. A. DeWolfe. *The Atlantic Monthly and Its Makers.* Boston: Atlantic Monthly Press, 1919.

Howells, William Dean. "Editor's Study." *Harper's Weekly.* January 1888, 154.

———. "Editor's Study" *Harper's Magazine,* LXXXI (September, 1890: 639–640).

———. "On Truth in Fiction," in George Becker, ed., *Documents of Modern Literary Realism.* Princeton: Princeton UP, 1963.

———. *A Hazard of New Fortunes,* New York: Meridian Classic, 1983.

———. *Literature and Life.* New York: Harpers, 1901.

———. "An Elder America." *The Nation* v.3 (2887) November 3, 1920.

———. "Editor's Study." *Harper's New Monthly Magazine* 78(February 1889), 488.

———. "In Honor of Tolstoy," *Critic,* XXX (October, 1898).

———. "The Man of Letters as a Man of Business," in Howells, *Literature and Life.*

———. "The Man of Letters as a Man of Business." in *Literature and Life,* Harper: New York & London, 1902.

———. *A Hazard of New Fortunes.* New York: Harper & Brothers, 1911.

———. *Criticism and Fiction and Other Essays,* edited by Clara Marburg Kirk and Rudolph Kirk. New York: NYU Press, 1959.

———. *Imaginary Interviews.* New York, London: Harper & Brothers, 1910.

———. *Literature and Life,* Harper: New York & London, 1902.

———. *The Vacation of the Kelwyns.* New York: Harper & Brothers, 1920.

———. *Years of My Youth.* Harper and Brothers: New York, 1916. pg. 226.

———. "Editor's Study" *Harper's New Monthly Magazine* 78 (February 1889), 488.

James, Henry. "William Dean Howells," *Harper's Weekly* 30 (19 June 1886): 394–95.

Johnson, Laura K. "Courting Justice : Marriage, Law, and the American Novel, 1890–1925." Diss., 2002.

Kirk and Kirk, *Howells.* American Book Company: New York, 1950.

Kirk, Clara Marburg. *William Dean Howells and Art in his Time,* New Brunswick: Rutgers UP, 1965.

Knoper, Randall. "American Literary Realism and Nervous 'Reflexion.'" *American Literature* 74.4 (2002): 715–45.

Lanum George, C. "Setting the Hook of Realism : A Study of the Early Career of William Dean Howells." 2002.

Ludwig, Sèami. Pragmatist Realism: The Cognitive Paradigm in American Realist Texts. Madison, WI: U of Wisconsin P, 2002.

Ludwig, Sèami. "The Realist Trickster as Legba: Howells's Capitalist Critique." *Mosaic: A Journal for the Interdisciplinary Study of Literature* 34.1 (2001): 173–84.

Lynn, Kenneth. *William Dean Howells, An American Life*. New York: Harcourt Brace, 1970.

Madison, Charles A. *Book Publishing in America*. New York: McGraw-Hill Book Company, 1966.

Marias, Julian. *Philosophy as Dramatic Theory*. University Park: Pennsylvania State UP, 1971.

McDermott, John J. ed., *The Writings of William James*. New York: Modern Library, 1968.

McLean, Ruari. *Modern Book Design from William Morris to the Present Day*. London: Faber & Faber, 1958.

Meserve, Walter J. *The Complete Plays of William Dean Howells*. New York: NYU Press, 1960.

Mitchell, Edward P. *Memoirs of an Editor*. New York: Alfred A. Knopf, 1924.

Moore, John Hammond. *Wiley, one hundred and seventy five years of publishing*. New York: Wiley, 1982.

Morgan, Charles. *The House of Macmillan*. London: Macmillan & Company, 1944.

Mott, Frank Luther. *Golden Multitudes: The Story of Best Sellers in the United States*. New York: Macmillan Company, 1947.

Munford, Howard, introduction to Nordloh and Kleinmann, eds., *The Minister's Charge*. Bloomington: University of Indiana Press, 1978. pp. xi–xxvi.

Nettles, Elsa. *Language, Race, and Social Class in Howells's America*. Lexington: University Press of Kentucky, 1988.

Pease, Donald, ed., *New Essays on the Rise of Silas Lapham*. Cambridge: Cambridge UP, 1991.

Perry, R.B. . *The Thought and Character of William James. The Thought and Character of William James*. Boston: Little, Brown & Co., 1935.

Pizer, Donald, "Introduction: The Problem of Definition." *The Cambridge Companion to American Realism and Naturalism*. Cambridge, New York: Cambridge University Press, 1995.

Pizer, Donald. "Crane Reports Garland on Howells," *Modern Language Notes*, LXX (January, 1955): 37–39.

Rubin, Lance Allen. "Remembering Is Hell": William Dean Howells, Realism, and the American Memory Crisis. microform, 2002.

Schlesinger, Arthur, Jr. "Anguish of a New York Liberal." *New York Review of Books* 49.2 (2002): 39–40.

Schweighauser, Philipp. "'You Must Make Less Noise in Here, Mister Schouler': Acoustic Profiling in American Realism." *Studies in American Fiction* 30.1 (2002): 85–102.

Seeyle, John. "The Hole in Howells/The Lapse in *Silas Lapham*." in Pease, *New Essays on the Rise of Silas Lapham*. Pp. 43–77.

Shaw, Ralph R. *Literary Property in the United States*. New York: Scarecrow Press, 1950.

Smith, Henry Nash and William M. Gibson. *Mark Twain—Howells's Letters*. 2 vols. Cambridge: Belknap Press of Harvard University Press, 1960.

Tebbel, John William Tebbel John William History of book publishing in the United States. *Between covers: The rise and transformation of book publishing in America*. New York: Oxford University Press, 1987.

The Atlantic Index Supplement, 1889–1901. Boston: Houghton, Mifflin, and Company, 1918.

The Atlantic Index. Boston: Houghton, Mifflin, & Company, 1889.

Trachtenberg, Alan. The Incorporation of America, Culture and Society in the Gilded Age. New York: Hill and Wang, 1982.

Webster, Samuel C. *Mark Twain: Business Man*. Boston: Little, Brown and Company, 1946.

Wilcox, Marrion. "The Works of William Dean Howells," *Harper's Weekly* 40 (4 July 1896): 655.

Wild, James. *The Radical Empiricism of William James*. New York: Doubleday & Co., 1969.

Wilshire, Bruce W. ed. . *William James, The Essential Writings*. Albany: SUNY Press, 1983.

Yard, Robert Sterling. *The Publisher*. Boston: Houghton Mifflin Company, 1913.

Index

NEWTON COUNTRY DAY SCHOOL
785 CENTRE STREET
NEWTON, MA 02458